BOBBY CHARLTON'S BOOK

of EUROPEAN FOOTBALL

Number 3

Foreword by Bill Shankly

The Star Team

GORDON BANKS

SHAY BRENNAN   BOBBY MONCUR

BILL SHANKLY   FRANK McLINTOCK   SIR MATT BUSBY

GORDON HILL   PIETRO ANASTASI   FRANZ HASIL   DRAGAN DZAJIC

TED MACAULEY

SOUVENIR PRESS LTD • *LONDON*

First published by Souvenir Press Ltd., 95 Mortimer Street, London, W.1, and simultaneously in Canada by J. M. Dent & Sons Ltd., Ontario

ISBN. 0.285.62015.0

Printed in Great Britain by GILMOUR & DEAN LTD., Hamilton and London.

CONTENTS

Bobby Charlton in action in London.

List of Illustrations

A grimace from Cyril Knowles as Pat Jennings clears in an FA Cup tie against Nottingham Forest at White Hart Lane.

BOBBY—HE'S JUST GREAT

FEWER things have given me greater pleasure than being afforded the opportunity to associate myself with Bobby Charlton in his European Football Book.

We have been friends for a long time, so much so that even on a Saturday morning, when Liverpool have been playing Manchester United at Old Trafford, I have gone round to Bobby's home for a cup of tea before the game. And I have always been made welcome.

I first saw him playing for Northumberland Boys when he was a stripling. I was the manager of a small club then and the likes of Charlton were just not for me. We had no youth policies.

But I remember being at Maine Road seeing him for the first time and wondering who would be after him. I got my answer in a few short minutes. When I looked round there was Matt Busby and Louis Edwards, from Manchester United, of course. And Bobby went their way.

It's old hat to list his achievements and I won't do it. But I'd just like to say that he deserves every single one of them. He's been honest and fair in his approach to football and, I am certain, has never cheated in his life. That's the mark of not only the player but the man, too.

I have three methods of training and handling men at Anfield. The hammer, the whip and the gentle word. Bobby would never need any of them. He's a phenomenon. He has so many tremendous qualities and skills that it is impossible to single out only one. But if I had to, I'd say his greatest quality is his honesty. That makes a man what he is. That's what has made Charlton the most loved name in football.

Liverpool sta[r]
Steve Heighwa[y]
challenged by Burn-
ley's Colin Wal-
dron.

Juggling George! A typical action shot of Georgie Best in full cry.

Bobby shows he can do a bit, too. Coventry 'keeper Bill Glazier lies helpless as the Manchester United captain dummies his way into position for a scoring shot.

THERE is one theme shared by just about every contributor to my book and it is this: there is no place like Europe to provide soccer excitement.

My boss Sir Matt Busby, back briefly in the manager's seat at Old Trafford, Bill Shankly, the Liverpool genius who steered his side into the FA Cup Final, and Frank McLintock, Arsenal's fine skipper, all agree that the matching of the best that is British against the tops in Europe is thrilling for both the fans and the footballers alike.

With this book I have notched another hat-trick—it's the third European Football Book I have written and recapturing some of the past season's tingling moments and reliving the memories of its stars, even if I myself was not playing in the great foreign competitions, has given me enormous pleasure.

When I toured Australia in summer 1970, right after the World Cup in Mexico, I saw enough enthusiasm among the youngsters Down Under to make me believe that the greatest game ever devised is getting a hold even in places far removed from the so-called centres of the sport, Europe and England.

Wherever I went, as you can see in the picture taken before the Hakoah versus Hellenicos match at Wentworth Park, I was mobbed by keen little ones anxious to show that the Aussies know what it's all about.

It was thrilling for me to visit them and watch their efforts; it made up for the dreadful disappointments in Mexico with England.

There can be no doubt that soccer horizons extend even further afield than Europe and South America.

Bobby Charlton.

THE MAN WHO MADE IT TO WEMBLEY

Alun Evans of Liverpool was a late choice for their FA Cup final team and was replaced during the game by substitute Peter Thompson.

...AND THE MAN WHO JUST MISSED ▶

A typical piece of challenging action from Stoke City's Terry Conroy who saw his Cup medal go in a semi-final defeat by Arsenal.

...obby and Sir Alf Ramsey as the England schemer is pulled from the fray in England's World Cup knock-out game with West Germany.

MY WORLD CUP STORY

By
Bobby
Charlton

> **When Sir Alf Ramsey pulled me off the pitch during England's World Cup match against West Germany I felt as upset as I have been about anything in my career.**
>
> **We were leading 2–0, and looking all over winners, when I got the signal to go off. The awful thing was that up to then I felt on top of the world; I wasn't tired and I felt as if I could go on playing all night, I was so much on top of my fitness that the game was no effort.**

I KNOW that quite a few people have used me as an excuse for what was to turn into a terrible defeat at the hands of the West Germans. But, quite honestly, I don't think I would have made all that difference to the situation. And I feel that if I had been Sir Alf I would have done the same.

It was hard for me to be as objective as Sir Alf when he pulled me off; but, after a while, I realised that he was probably saving me for the semi-finals in Mexico City.

He thought, like we all did, that the game was as good as won and with the semi-finals, a very difficult task, lying ahead he was already planning his moves. The semi-final was going to be tough if only because it was going to be played three or four thousand feet higher than we had been playing.

We all knew in the England team that substitutes would be widely used and that none of us, whoever he was, could guarantee that he would be on the park for the whole 90 minutes of any game. With conditions as they were, with so much difficulty in breathing, this had to be the situation.

After I had swallowed my disappointment I began to realise that if I was being saved for Mexico City it was a wise move.

I'm afraid it didn't lessen the frustration as I sat and watched our lead being whittled away until it had finally disappeared and the Germans had won. Sitting there, being able to do nothing to halt the slide, was a terribly agonising experience.

THE MAN WHO MADE IT THE HARD WAY

Jimmy Greaves pictured arriving in Mexico City after driving there in a rally.

But, it seemed to me, it was fate that the Germans were winning. England, I felt, had not played better all the time we were in Mexico and when we went two-up it seemed only fair reward for the excellence of our play and our determination.

Even now I am convinced that England could have won the World Cup; I didn't believe the Germans deserved to beat us and now, on reflection, I still don't.

I would bet that when they trooped off the field at the end they were asking themselves: "What happened? How did we do it? How did we manage to score three goals?"

I know that's what I was pondering. Fate seemed to be the only answer. There was no other apparent reason. None of the lads played badly, nobody made any mistakes, it was simply that the ball began to fall at the right place at the right time for the Germans.

When Beckenbauer scored it was with a shot that could hardly have made him satisfied. He probably thought as it left his boot: "Ah, well, I'll have to try and do better next time."

But there it was in the back of the net. It went into a no man's land so far as Peter Bonetti was concerned and he couldn't cut it out.

The second, by Uwe Seeler, was just as lucky. When he jumped to get the ball I think he tried to head it back for one of his team mates behind him as he stood at the far post. Instead it caught the back of his head and went right over everybody into the top corner. It took him a few seconds to find out what had happened to it. He got the answer when the Germans rushed across to congratulate him. And they were level. It was unbelievable.

It was an impossible goal, really. But there it was in the net with the England boys looking dumfounded. You can imagine what a boost it was to the Germans with only something like five minutes to go to full-time. It had the opposite effect on us.

Muller got the third in extra-time from a centre that had been knocked back into the middle. It dropped at his feet a few yards out and he didn't fail; but it was the only thing he had done all afternoon.

Everything looked black because West Germany

WORLD
CUP
ACTION

licked us when they had a few minutes of really good luck. But, had we won 2–0, we would have gone into the semi-finals against Italy, a team we didn't fear at all.

Imagine how we would have fared with all the room and freedom that they gave the Germans in the semi-final. I just could not see us failing to get to the final—and we would have surely given the Brazilians a better, tougher game than the Italians did.

In fact, if you'd asked Brazil who they would rather have met in the final they would have said Italy. We were much more composed in our play, our mental attitude was right and we were very much on top of things. Brazil had had a difficult time in beating us in the qualifying round and I am sure they had a great regard for our skill.

I am sure that with only two games to go to achieve what we had achieved in 1966 we would not have let the chance slip away. Even in defeat we all still felt that we were as good a side as either of the two in the final and most certainly good enough to beat Brazil in a quick death situation.

That chance has gone and we must look forward to Munich. By then Sir Alf will have tried around 100 players at all sorts of levels; full International, Under-23, Football League and all sorts of representative matches. He will be looking for young blood, of course. New men to carry our hopes. But if he thinks I can do a job for him he will, I'm sure, pick me even though I will be 36.

We will still be the side to beat in 1974 with the Brazilians, the West Germans, and despite their final failure, the Italians. The Italians, I think, learned something from their final appearance in the Mexico World Cup. They will put it all to good use in their build-up to Munich.

The time in between will be interesting. They will be a side to watch in this run-in to the world championships.

Throughout 1970 and 1971 they underwent a vast re-think on their game. Suddenly they decided

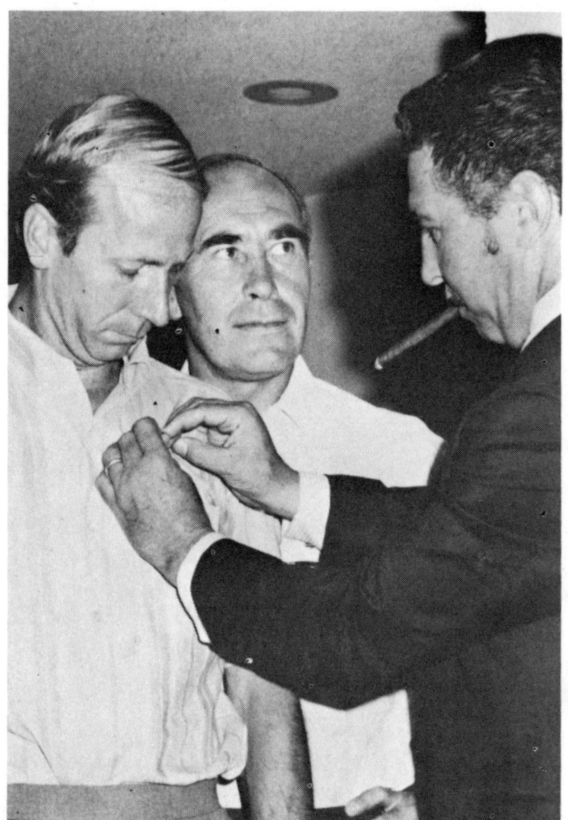

Bobby gets a medal and Sir Alf gets a halo.

THE ENGLAND PARTY COLLECT THEIR WORLD CUP CARS ON LOAN FROM FORDS.

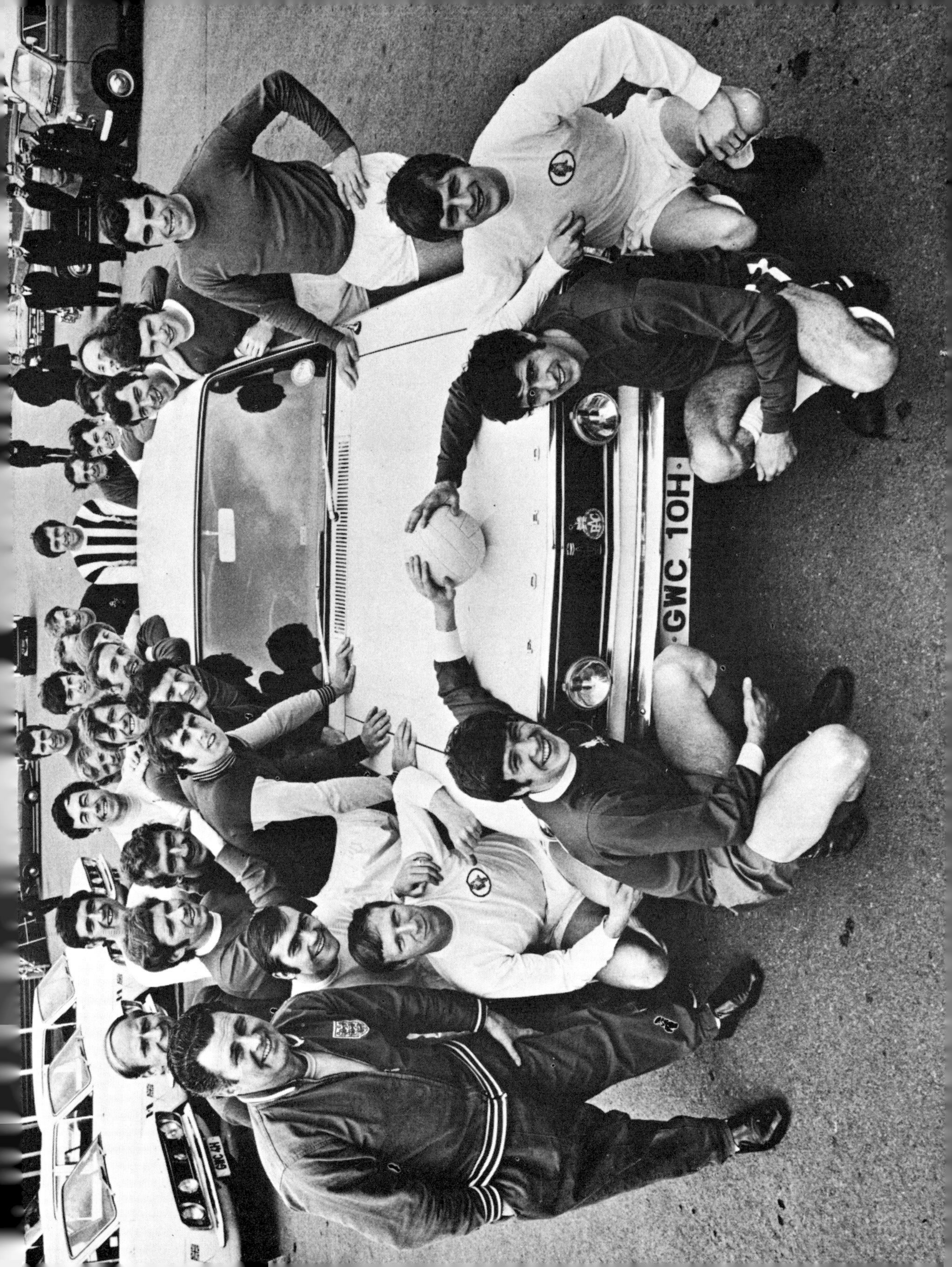

Coates, the man who had to come home. . . ."

that goals were the thing and abandoned the old ideas of ultra-strong defensive systems that were boring for players and spectators alike.

On a couple of trips to Italy early in 1971 I saw results that would have been unheard of a year before; teams were winning by three and four clear goals and forwards were shooting from all over the place.

It showed me that they were trying hard to revolutionise their game and draft in some English ideas. I was really impressed, they had made the game go faster and tried very hard to organise more goal scoring chances.

They tried, too, to eliminate the petty fouling and terrible displays of dissent which had always been a feature of their game.

The Italians were disappointed that they fell at the last hurdle in the World Cup and designed a complete overhaul of their soccer scene to fit in with modern ideas. Part of the plan was to organise the Anglo-Italian league to get a closer look at more aspects of the English style of play.

Many people thought they could be THE side of the World Cup 1970. I think they were a little too early. But they could be THE side of the World Cup 1974.

Referee **GORDON HILL** is fearless, respected by footballers everywhere and destined to become one of the great characters of the European soccer scene. His ambition is to become a FIFA referee. Here, he tells of the sort of problems he has already encountered in three football capitals abroad.

EUROPEAN WHISTLE STOP

DATELINE: Madrid. The noise, when you emerge from the dark tunnel and march onto the floodlit splendour of Real Madrid's Bernabeau Stadium, can best be described as an explosion of sound; it sends your ears rippling and your heart beating wildly.

When it's the roar of welcome for two teams and the officials before the game it is a stirring experience; when it gives way to the deafening howl of derision it is a blood-curdling sensation. An unforgettable nightmare of noise.

This, in 1968, my first ever trip abroad as an official, was the baptism I was afforded at this great citadel of soccer tradition. I was linesman with Tommy McKitterick and with Jim Finney as referee for the Real Madrid versus Sparta Prague European Cup quarter-final first-leg.

23

IMPLACABLE

That's Kevin Howley, pictured as he listens to a plea from Manchester City's Colin Bell with Francis Lee running to add his weight to the argument.

AMIABLE

That's FIFA referee Jim Finney watching with Brian Labone as the Everton trainer treats goalkeeper Gordon West.

UNSHAKEABLE

That's referee John Homewood, of Sunbury, as he talks to Manchester United's George Best after an incident in which Manchester City full back Glyn Pardoe suffered a broken leg.

We had been treated to two magnificent days of all that is best in Spanish hospitality; we were VIPs, lauded, pampered and fussed over at every stride we took in the capital.

Nothing was too much trouble; we had only to ask and whatever we wanted to do or see was immediately taken care of. It was, for those few short days, an unforgettable period of my life as an official.

In my suitcase was an inscribed gold watch for me from Real Madrid and another to give to my wife Audrey when I got home.

The lavishness of the gifts we all received was matched only by the absolute kindness shown by the officials of the club who were determined to make our trip as memorable as they could; and for me, on my first football trip to Europe, it spelt out all that I had dreamed about.

There were 125,000 fanatical Spanish supporters towering in terraces above us as Jim, Tommy and I, in front of the two teams, began our ceremonial march towards the centre of the pitch for the preliminaries.

Flashlights popped; photographers scurried round and elbowed each other aside for the best pictures; television camera teams from all over Europe, except Britain, radio commentators and scores of officials crowded round as we made our way out.

And I recall Jim Finney's sobering words that came like a cold water spray to make sure we hadn't been over-impressed by the VIP treatment: "Remember, lads, this is why we came."

Within five minutes of the start I certainly knew I was in the game: I flagged Gento, the Real left winger and captain, for offside. I was right up with him, running as quickly as he was and probably faster than the full-back who was marking him, so I knew I was right.

My red flag shot up into the air—and it was the signal for all the hatred of the Real fans to be directed at me. There were jeers and whistles and a great buzz of objection. Gento, who had always been an idol of mine from seeing him play against Manchester United at Old Trafford, came across to me and began to wave his arms about and gabble excitedly about my decision.

I fenced him off with the stick part of the flag and finally pushed him away. It was like touching a god—the crowd couldn't believe their eyes.

Then, from the perpendicular heights that housed the crowd, the sky was suddenly thick with leaves of fire. Irate fans set fire to pages of newspapers and sent them spiralling down towards me; flaming leaves, sooty and downright dangerous when they fluttered, still burning, close to me. But I thought the best thing to do was keep moving.

But now, more than I could plan, I felt I was deeply involved in the game; I was as much part of it as the players. I began to enjoy the tension, began to feed on it. And, even though I was a little afraid, I began to enjoy that sensation, too.

If my flagging of Gento hadn't been bad enough Jim Finney sent them all wild when he disallowed a goal by Amancio after about ten minutes. The Real ace had been fouled, but he staggered on, got himself balanced and cracked home a beautiful goal from something like 20 yards out.

Neither he, nor I for that matter, had heard Jim's whistle shrill for a free kick for the foul. But, even when the ball was sending the net billowing, there was Jim, cool and phlegmatic, doggedly pointing to the spot where the free kick was to be taken from.

Amancio went into a rage—so did the rest of his team-mates. And, down from the crowd, more fiery leaves came fluttering down like a very hot autumn. But Jim stuck to his decision. It must have taken him at least five minutes to get the game re-started but, somehow, he managed it. Even now the thought of dis-allowing what would have been their first goal in such an important game sends me cold.

By half-time, still keeping pace with Gento along the left wing, I had flagged the Real favourite offside another four or five times. And fenced him off with my stick. I don't think we were the three most popular Britons in the world when half-time loomed.

And when Jim Finney signalled that first half was over I dashed from the other side of the pitch to join him and Tommy for what seemed like a ten mile walk to our changing room. In fact it was about 100 yards—but it was a gauntlet of anger with

Alan Mullery, Tony Dunne and Bobby Charlton in action at Old Trafford.

people shouting all sorts of things at us.

Jim hissed under his breath: "Stick together, lads, stick together." And shoulder-to-shoulder, showing Britain's pride at every step, we strode towards the haven of our little room.

When we got in we all sighed: "Phew." And I stood with my back jammed against the door while we drank our tea. For ten minutes we examined what we should do and Jim, an old campaigner, summed it up simply by saying: "We must go on showing courage. We are right. The laws of the game are on our side."

It wasn't too much comfort under the circumstances—but it was all we had. We were all alone; and we were probably the only men in the stadium who were ice-cold in the heat.

In the second-half I took the Sparta attack so I wasn't matching Gento for his speed any longer; the game settled down into a good contest and Real ran out 3–0 winners. Manchester United went on to beat them in the semi-finals to become the first English club to win the European Cup.

I had been to Spain working as a liaison man with the Education Corps when I was stationed with the army at Gibraltar. My trips then were nothing like as memorable or as hectic as this one. But I wouldn't have missed it for the world.

Dateline: Berlin. The superb Olympic Stadium, built by Hitler, was the impressive stage for the match that earned me my second soccer trip abroad.

Once again, by sheer coincidence, I was teamed up with Jim Finney who was to referee the game between Hertha (Berlin) and Vitoria Setubal, from Portugal.

Hertha and Setubal had drawn 1–1 in the first leg of the third round of the Fairs Cup and the second leg was to be fought out in West Berlin. But what a night!

It was in Berlin that I began to believe that things seem to happen whenever I'm around. It's not that there was any trouble, nor were there any disputed decisions or controversial actions. But conditions were worse than I have ever seen anywhere; for a start it was 30 degrees below freezing. And that's pretty cold.

When we got to the ground the pitch was three or four feet deep in snow; ground staff cleared some of it away but they couldn't move it all from the pitch because to pile it up at the side would have meant that the spectators wouldn't have been able to see. There was that much of it.

Instead they rolled it flat—and the game went on. But how the Portuguese players managed to survive, let alone play, I'll never know. Most of them were from Mozambique and were used to the warm, sultry African heat.

They had never even seen snow before and were romping about like happy schoolchildren before the game rubbing each other's faces in snowballs. But when they had to strip down to soccer gear for the game they were far from happy.

They stood around when they were not involved with hands thrust into gloves and with teeth chattering like the sound effects department of a film studio recording a cavalry charge on hard ground!

The German side decided to wear black tights under their shorts and when I got a whiff of the outside temperature I asked Jim Finney if he'd mind if I wore a pair to keep me warm. He agreed —and off I went to borrow a pair.

But when I took a look at myself and realised what a twit I looked in them I decided I'd rather freeze. I'm not so sure it was the wisest decision I'd ever made. By half-time I couldn't feel my fingers, I could hardly hold the flag and the pain, from the cold, was almost too much to bear.

Somebody let me borrow a pair of enormous woolly mittens for the second half and I ran the line wearing them; the first time I've ever given in to the weather. But even then, by the time the final whistle went, I was ill with the cold.

Those lads from Setubal must have been really brave to put up with it; they lost 1–0, but I'm sure they just wanted to get the game over and done with before they froze to a complete standstill.

One of them—I don't know his name—went headlong over the touchline and vanished into a four foot deep mound of snow and ice; all I could see were his legs threshing about, the only part of him showing from the snow pile.

Nobody could leave the pitch to help him—Jim was yelling: "Play on." Somehow the lad struggled

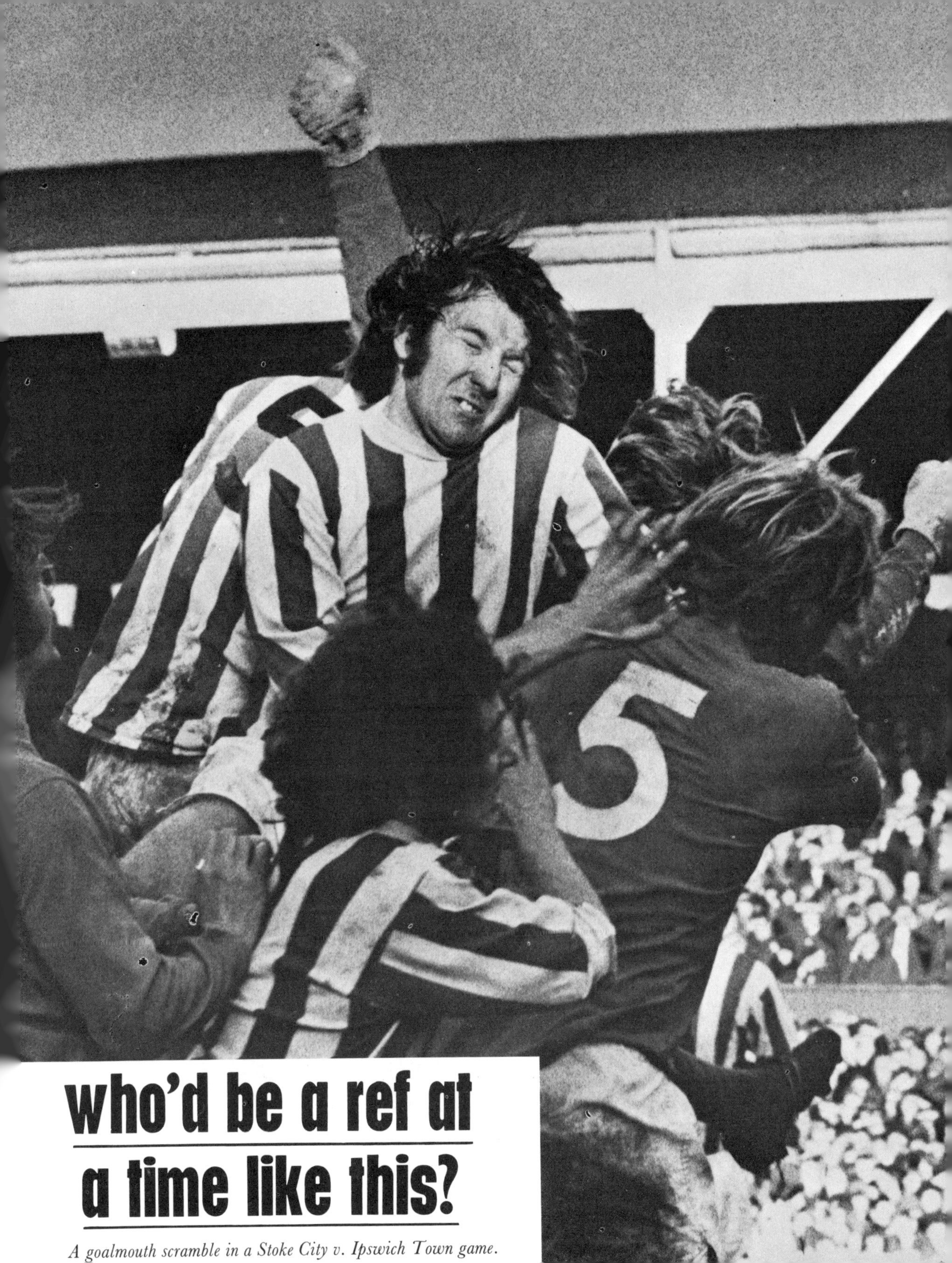

who'd be a ref at a time like this?

A goalmouth scramble in a Stoke City v. Ipswich Town game.

"I wonder who they're talking about." Johnny Morrissey, Joe Royle and Alan Ball in the picture.

clear and got back into the game.

Dateline: Rome. On my third trip abroad I, at long last, was in control of the game. I was the referee appointed to officiate at the Anglo-Italian league game between Lazio and Wolverhampton Wanderers.

The venue was the absolutely beautiful Olympic stadium with it's classical statues of the ancient Roman gods lined up along the top of the terracing. They were the silent witnesses when I sent off the Lazio goalkeeper . . .

The game at Wolverhampton had been, shall we say, a little heated. And, at the end, the police had locked both teams in the dressing rooms to prevent further trouble. It was with this happy knowledge that I flew off to Rome for the group three match in summer 1970.

There were only about 25,000 Italians in the ground—but even such a comparatively small gathering is worth a crowd of 100,000 any where else in the world. They make so much noise.

And this was no exception; there were fireworks and rockets flying off all over the place when the game got underway.

It was as if the whole world had gone soccer crazy. After the calm before the match, when I had been shown all over the lovely city, looking at Michael Angelo's historic work at almost every turn, the atmosphere in the stadium was ear-splitting.

The game was moving along reasonably happily, with not too much for me to worry my head about, when Derek Dougan suddenly grabbed me, spun me round and yelled: "Look, Gordon, the linesman's flagging like mad back there."

He pointed down the pitch and I could see Bobby Bell's flag wagging insistently. A few yards away from him I noticed a Wolves forward stretched full-length along the turf, apparently senseless and certainly impervious to the furore going on around his prostrate figure.

There was no obvious culprit. The goalkeeper, a large fellow with shoulders that looked as if they had a milk-yoke balanced on them under his jersey, was standing on his line looking innocent.

Bobby Bell, however, had seen him rush from his goal and uppercut the Wolves man with as classical a punch as any of the athletic gods could have managed with their marble fists.

I hadn't seen the action—but Bobby was such a good linesman that I had to act on his information. I asked him: "What shall I do, then?" with one eye on the roaring crowd.

He answered: "He'll have to go. You'll have to send him off." I strode over to the goalkeeper and demanded his name.

"Michael Angelo . . ." he said as I got my book and pencil out. That was too much for me. His action had been bad enough in flooring the Wolves man—and now he was taking the mickey. He just had to go. And I sent him off.

It was only after the game—which ended a few minutes later—that I discovered his name really was Michael Angelo . . . That name, it seemed, was haunting me on my trip to Rome.

He was only the second player I had dismissed in my career; the other man had been sent off in my first season as a ref., in 1962, but before I got onto the League list.

It spoiled what would have been a happy memory of my first international appointment as a referee. But it was inevitable.

I don't like sending players off; nor do I like booking them unless it's absolutely necessary and there is no other way out. I prefer to sort things out in my own fashion.

The experiences I have had in Europe have given me an insatiable appetite for more involvement in soccer abroad and it's my ambition to get onto the FIFA list. The players love to go into Europe—and it's the same with the referees. It's the tops. It's the very acme of football to be in charge of first-class European competition games and that's where I aim to be.

I would dearly love to take over from Jim Finney controlling the best games in Europe.

Stoke agony as Mike Bernard hits a miss.

Colchester ecstasy as Ray Crawford scores in the Leeds Cup k.o.

A RED STAR

By Dragan Dzajic (Red Star Belgrade)

IT was a case of listening to the old, old story. Playing for Yugoslavia against Belgium in a qualifying match for the recent World Cup, I was provoked by a Belgian defender, tried to keep my temper, failed and was sent off. From the moment I stepped onto the pitch I knew I was in for one of those matches—the sort of match in which one or two or three of the opposing team have been detailed to stop me at all costs. But that can never excuse my retaliation, and sitting in the dressing-rooms by myself as the match progressed I realised how stupid I had been. No player ever helped a team to win from a bench in the dressing-room.

But the problem remains. I'm not entirely convinced that referees protect star players as much as they should. I'm something of an oddity in the modern game—the orthodox winger who likes to dribble the ball round the back of a defence. Of course, I like to cut in and score goals, but for me there is nothing more dangerous than the player who breaks open one side of a defence and puts over a precision centre behind the opposition's defensive line.

Give me a fullback who plays fair and I'm satisfied. I'll try him to one side, then the next, probing for his weaknesses. When I think I've found them, I'll be off, straight at him, confident in the knowledge that he can be beaten.

But what about the players who come in really

"Denis Law was among the Manchester United stars who were at the height of their powers when George Best came into the team"

hard, aiming for your legs rather than for the ball. These fellows make me very annoyed. If they can't tackle, they shouldn't be playing as fullbacks. If they're put there to act as a deterrent, then that is foul tactics on the part of the team manager or coach, a deliberate attempt to intimidate the opposition. It isn't football.

I have come to accept rough treatment as part and parcel of the game, just another factor that I have to cope with. The reason for it lies in the past. I began playing football with a small Yugoslavian team, Jedinstvo Ub and was transferred to Red Star of Belgrade when I was only sixteen. A year later I made my debut in the Red Star team.

Red Star of Belgrade are probably the most famous team in Yugoslavia and from the start I was fortunate. When I came into the first team there were many players still in the game who had contributed to Yugoslavia's success in the 1962 World Cup in Chile. And in the Red Star team I found myself alongside players such as Kostic, Sekularac, Durkovic, Popovic. These were the men who helped my game to develop quickly. There is an analogy here with, say, George Best. He came into the Manchester United team when players such as Bobby Charlton, Denis Law, Pat Crerand were at the height of their powers. He came into a winning team, which meant that his great gifts were able to develop quickly and were helped by the play of those around him.

This meant that I was soon in contention for a place in the national team, and this was duly awarded to me. Soon after I was made captain of Red Star, the following year, captain of the Yugoslavian national team. I have won over four dozen caps for my country, have played over 400 games for Red Star, won four championship medals and three cup medals.

The point of this is to show that from the age of seventeen onwards, as a winger in the modern game, I have been subjected to some bad tackling. In many countries the winger has tended to fade from the scene in the last few years. The reasons are obvious to most people, but it is sometimes hard to decide which came first—whether teams played without wingers from tactical reasons, or whether

the wingers who played simply weren't good enough for their national teams.

Possibly the latter reason is one that has been overlooked. It's a chain effect, of course, so that as soon as teams decided to do without wingmen, the younger players coming up in the game had to change their style of play. I've always seen my job as being one of teamwork. The winger can do all the brilliant dribbling in the world, he can sprint around the pitch and make fools of the opposing defence, but all his work is wasted unless he gets the ball across into the middle both accurately and swiftly.

This is possibly the reason why many teams do without wingers. The players are there, but so often their finishing work is below standard. These are players with magical footwork, they can beat their fullback by turning on all the tricks in their repertoire, but the final cross when it comes is often too deep or too shallow, never seems to reach the feet or head of the player running in to score.

Someone once asked me the secret in the art of dribbling a fullback. My reply was that you have to make the fullback believe that two balls are in play. You leave him the imaginary one, and take the real one yourself. It's an art that you can learn and it takes a lot of training, a lot of patience to perfect the technique. But I find that when I train, I always want to do it with other players, get the feel of teamwork firmly into my play, make sure that there is always an end product to everything I do.

There was a nice contrast a few seasons ago when Yugoslavia played England in the European Nations Cup. Our team was largely unknown at the time, having been built up slowly over the previous years, not having played in the 1966 World Cup finals.

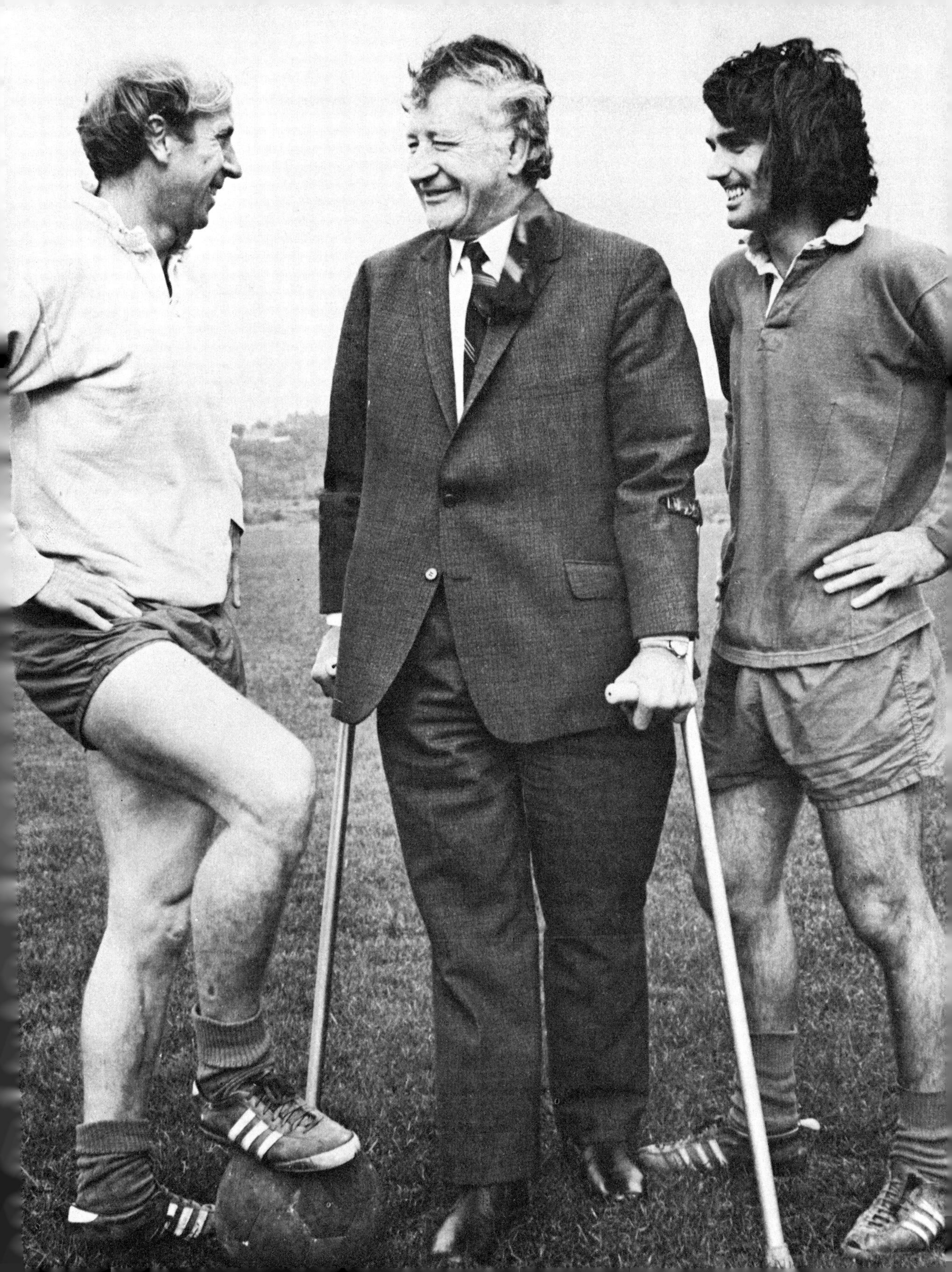

When we played England in Florence, it was obvious that many of the English players were exhausted after a hard season. But most important was the fact that we managed to get behind the English defence on the wings. I felt that we were unlucky not to win that tournament. We held Italy to a draw in the first final, only to lose the return match when we were tired.

Twice I have been chosen to play for "The World" selections. The first was in Rio in 1968, when I played for a team that lost by two goals to one against Brazil. Then in the winter of 1970 I played for a team of European players against Benfica of Portugal, a match in honour of the old Benfica captain, Coluna. For the past four years I have been the Yugoslavian Player of the Year. But the real thrill came last year when I was voted Sportsman of the Year as well.

How much longer will I stay in the game? At the moment, I can't say. But I will play as long as I enjoy playing and feel that I have something to offer. When that is over I will take advantage of the studies that I have been pursuing at university in my spare time. I feel that this is important. So many young players come into the game with nothing behind them in the way of training and often they are forced out of the game at an age when it is hard to find a suitable employment. It is therefore, important, I think, to pursue outside interests however enthusiastic you are about football. And I realise fully the good work being done by many clubs throughout Europe who arrange training schemes of various sorts for the younger players coming into the game.

So—I'll continue playing for, I hope, many years to come. And I hope also, that we shall see a uniformity in refereeing standards throughout the game. The stakes are so high now, the amount of money in the game is so vast, that it is inevitable that players should take games very keenly. But it also becomes imperative that refereeing standards remain high. If we let them slip just a little, they will slide away quickly and the basic nature of football will be ruined. So we come back again to my game, the play of the winger in modern football.

Something to laugh about as England teammates Alan Ball and Martin Peters collide.

EUROPE: THE GREAT GLORY

SIR MATT BUSBY, a pioneer into the European soccer scene and the father of Manchester United's glorious tradition, tells of the immense frustrations when there are no trophies to hunt.

MANCHESTER UNITED are an important part of European football and when we are absent from the front line of competition abroad it is a heartbreaking situation.

We looked towards the FA Cup competition as our last chance to get into Europe after Aston Villa had removed us from the League Cup in 1971.

Then, when Middlesbrough knocked us out of the FA Cup, we were suddenly left with nothing to go for; there were no trophies, no big prizes for Manchester United to chase and, what's more important, the door to Europe had been convincingly slammed in our faces.

I felt that not only were Manchester United being robbed of the glory their great traditions deserve but the continental public at large were also being starved of the chance of seeing three of the finest individual skills in soccer. I'm talking about Bobby Charlton, Denis Law and George Best, three players whose individual gifts of brilliance, in different aspects of the game, spark tremendous interest abroad.

In Britain the public seem to prefer unit success from a team with, of course, an appreciation of individual skills within the mould of the unit. But in Europe there is a much greater appreciation by the fans of individuality; they love the inventive flair of players like George Best, the electric dash of

Wilf McGuinness (right) and George Best.

ONE VITAL GOAL

Bobby Charlton scoring the last European goal at Old Trafford. It wasn't enough to pull United through the second leg of the European Cup Semi-final in season '68-'69. Inter-Milan had won at San Siro by 2-0.

Law and the smooth long passing of Bobby Charlton.

Manchester United, probably more than any other British team, provide this sort of spectacle. With three such players flamboyant football is inevitable. The fellow of exceptional skill is regarded with absolute awe and tremendous appreciation abroad.

We have been through a bad time, the worst for many a long year at Old Trafford, and when Middlesbrough put us out of the FA Cup I couldn't wait for the end of the season to come, even though it was still three months off.

I wanted desperately to get the season out of the way so that we may have another attempt at getting back where we belong—into Europe. And that's an aim that is always uppermost in our minds.

Whenever I heard an FA Cup draw or the matchings in the European Cup I felt it like I might feel a stab to the heart; I was sad, disappointed and terribly frustrated that we were out of everything and with only a respectable league placing to play for.

I certainly did not think we deserved to be beaten by Middlesbrough in that last chance for Europe bid. And, sometimes I think that when teams like Middlesbrough manage to beat a team like United they are often surprised at what they have achieved. I refuse to take anything away from Middlesbrough —they deserved to win because they were prepared to take greater risks than I would have liked my players to take in the dreadful conditions.

But, even now, I am convinced that in better conditions than the snow and ice Manchester United would have got through. It would have been a struggle, as it had been the year before, but we would have done it. Middlesbrough have managed to give us a tough time each time we have met them in successive seasons.

Of course I don't know how far we would have got in the FA Cup, even if we had beaten Middlesbrough, but it was, after all, the last straw we had to cling to and I am sure that having got through that round we would have been difficult to beat.

When I took over again as team manager from Wilf McGuinness, who, I am very sad to say, didn't make it I felt that I had to guard the great traditions of Manchester United. I felt they had been slipping away and I needed to arrest them. It was sad that the club was entering a bad time and that nothing we did seemed to be able to bring it clear.

The immense frustration I felt, and the disappointments we had when we tried to buy three or four new players and were turned down, only added to the general depression.

It was as if we needed a bridging loan on skill, somebody to help us through, I wanted not big name players—but players who had proved themselves, not men I would have to develop. I wanted a new skill—and one man, I think, would have helped us enormously—that I could draft into the side without a waiting period.

We had, and still have, of course, an immense store of young skill in the reserves and the "A" team—but, again, frustratingly they were too young. Too young to throw into the hurly-burly of top flight competition.

The future, I know, is secure with these brilliant youngsters; some of them, given a year or two on their age, would have been in the Manchester United side now. An established player or two would have bridged that gap between what we have now and what we will have in a few years time. This has been our problem at Old Trafford. The players I wanted, and the activity behind the scenes to get them was considerable, were just not available. The answer was always "No". Because we don't advertise our intentions all the time some fans tend to believe we are doing nothing; nothing could be further from the truth.

If these players I had wanted had become available they would have been bought.

Maybe by the time you read this they are already ours. The transfer market changes so quickly that it is impossible to make forecasts. All I can say is that there is plenty of money available to buy; but we want to buy right. We want to buy investments, men who are fit to play for Manchester United.

When I decided to take the job as general manager and support Wilf McGuinness in the team manager's job I was a tired man; I was physically worn out and ready to move over to allow the continuity of progress through Wilf to carry on.

Mentally I was on top form; but the rigours of all that goes with team managership were beginning to be too much for me. Obviously I didn't have the same sort of enthusiasm for the job that I'd had as a much younger man—and the increasing tiredness I felt made me feel the time was ripe for a handover to a younger man.

The stresses of a manager's job are seemingly without end. There's a lot to think about and you feel you can never escape it. Driving home in the car, sitting in the house, or in bed at night the problems of the day, the week or the month were constantly buzzing around my head.

It's history now that Wilf, to my regret, didn't make the success of the job that we felt he would. It's impossible to work out why, it's just one of those things.

But when I was general manager, and not so closely associated with the team as I had been as team boss, I became more like a supporter. I got really angry when we lost; I saw the game in an entirely different light. I was more critical and, like a supporter, frustrated when success didn't come. In short, I was a different person so far as football was concerned.

Again, at the time of writing, we haven't decided on who will assume the job of team boss but my legacy to him, when I move back into the general manager's chair, will be an assurance of a future rosy with the glow of young talent. He will have, too, as much money as he needs to build in his own players if he feels he wants to buy any. But the youngsters will be the lifeblood.

Europe is beckoning, as it always will for Manchester United. And we must answer the call. Even though the club has been levered out of Europe's top contests I am still in touch with feeling over there as a member of the European Technical Committee. Constantly, I am reminded on trips to the continent that United are sadly missed; and I am assured that they will be afforded an unforgettable welcome when, inevitably, they get back.

How terribly sad it is that a man who is as beloved, as skilful, as admired for his greatness as a player and as a man as Bobby Charlton is, should not be demonstrating his mastery in front of those great crowds. How sad, too, that Best and Law, are not in a position to make their eyes pop with admiration.

What of Bobby Charlton's future? This is a point I often ponder. I hope, of course, that he will still be playing for us for many years to come.

When his playing days are over he will not leave Manchester United if I have my way. His name is synonymous with Manchester United; it's just like two different ways of spelling the same thing. It's unthinkable to consider that he might ever be concerned with any other club.

He has too much to offer. He has opinions, which are good and sound. He has experience, a learned knowledge of the game and can handle men better than most. They are all excellent qualities.

A night out at the World Sporting Club, London.

JOHN TOSHACK

When Liverpool were knocked out of the FA Cup by Watford in 1969 manager Bill Shankly decided that the time had come to create a new Liverpool side.

Out went long established players . . . in came young men like John Toshack bought from Cardiff City to do the specialist job of taking and making chances created by fast raiding wing men.

In little more than a year the policy had matured. Liverpool were back at Wembley—but lost 2–1 in the final to Arsenal after a gruelling battle which went to extra-time.

B ILL SHANKLY'S contribution to football, both at home and abroad, has been one of memorable achievement for his beloved Liverpool. Stars in Europe and idols in one half of Merseyside, respected throughout football and feared as a unit, Shankly's scarlet shirted perfectionists survived the threat of transition and emerged with enough power to upset league pacemakers Leeds United and Arsenal at the crucial February run-in to the 1971 championship.

Shankly turned his back on history—and made a new future, built on the memory of the glory days, for Liverpool. He also began to build another challenge for Europe. And this is his background story. It's a warning light for those top continentals. . .

Rebuilding for Europe is the real aim

A S long ago as 1966, when we were leading the first division by six points and well on our way to winning the title, I could see the fabric of Liverpool's great side breaking up.

We were terrible in the last twelve games and it looked to me as if we were about to fall apart. I knew then that I would have to start re-building; that there would have to be a period of transition.

If everything had gone right for me in the transfer market the transitional time would have passed far more quickly and it would have been over and done with by 1970.

There were three, players I wanted, all defenders, but I couldn't get them. One of them even came to Anfield to see me and if I had had my way he would never have left. But circumstances wouldn't allow it; we didn't pay signing-on bonuses and these players wanted them.

As it turned out I had to start looking elsewhere and the change-over had to take a little longer.

The team I had then was great, a magnificent body of men, superb players and a team to be proud of; we had a mutual trust and a tremendous belief in each other.

It seemed to me then the every man on the field was an extension of me; they *were* me out there on the park. I knew instinctively what they were going to do—and they knew instinctively what I wanted them to do. It was as if I was there with them, playing alongside them. We were all on the same wavelength.

I don't think any manger can have had such an understanding with his team as I had with that side. Those great men who brought honour and satisfaction to me and to Liverpool were the finest Europe could produce. St. John, Yeats, Lawrence, Strong, Hunt. They were all tremendous.

Tommy Smith and Chris Lawler getting to grips with Allan Clarke, Leeds United. In the background, Bill Shankly's nomination for a future of fame—John McLaughlin. "Mark the name well—McLaughlin", says the Liverpool boss.

Ray Clemence, England's next 'keeper?

Ron Davies, John McLaughlin, Brian Hall and Jimmy Gabriel.

And it was heartbreaking that they should have to be split up; but they were getting too old. Young blood had to be brought in. I had to revitalise Liverpool.

I am guided by my conscience; I do what I think is honest and always have done from being a schoolboy. I expect honesty from men in my team because honesty breeds trust. And that way every player knows his teammate will be as involved as he is, he knows that there will be no shirking of duty, no relaxing of effort, no expecting somebody to do it for him. That's honesty at work in a football team.

And that, in short, was the basis of that fine team of mine. Now I'm building up the same sort of feeling in the new boys, the players who will have to fill those magnificent shirts with the same feel for pride and tradition that their predecessors did.

Slowly, but surely, they are doing it. Heighway, Hall, Toshack, Clemence, Lloyd. They'll all make it.

If any team is going to be a big name in football in Europe it's going to be Liverpool, and with a captain and player like Tommy Smith in their midst it would be difficult for them to fail.

Smith is exactly what I have always wanted him to be—a fierce competitor and a thorough professional with a will to win that matches my own. He hates to lose. So do I. He, more than them all, is an extension of me on the pitch.

I feel dreadful in defeat, awful. It's like a blow to my heart. When Swansea beat us in the FA Cup at Anfield—2–1 in the sixth round in the 1963–64 season—it was a national tragedy for Liverpool's supporters. I, too, will never forget it. I felt cheated, just as I always do in defeat.

When you have planned, and checked and had a re-think and planned again until you feel you have considered every eventuality, and you still lose, you can only feel cheated.

I would never take anything away from a good side who beat us fair and square; I don't crib if a team takes its chances and whacks us. If the referee has been fair, if we've had a fair crack of the whip

50

and my players have been honest in their effort then you'll never hear any grumbles from me.

We didn't spend time moaning then; we went on to win the first division championship. We turned a national tragedy to our advantage.

Many players would always prefer to win the FA Cup. It has that little bit of glamour. I prefer to win the league. That's the real test. A test of endurance. Of consistency. And fitness.

Wembley, of course, is the big occasion in English football. The players love it. It's the focal point of football in this country. And that's why I think it should have another use on Cup Final day.

I think that at half-time, when the two final teams are in the dressing rooms, the First Division championship trophy and the medals should be given in great ceremony to the team that has topped the league.

The English champions, I think, deserve that little bit of extra glory that Wembley would give them. The players should be paraded out in their civilian clothes, their club suits, and led up to receive their honour.

If the championship trophy can't be presented at the home ground—and the two times we won it we had away matches to close the season—then what better time or occasion than the Wembley cup final? It could be seen on television. The team could be applauded by a crowd of 100,000 football supporters who would be glad to cheer the champions of England instead of listening to that band.

Can you imagine the feeling it would give to the players? They would be on top of the world. Wembley and Cup Final day could become an even greater spectacle if this idea was adopted.

On the question of trophies I think that for any team to plan for the big four, the League, the FA and the League Cups and Europe, is unwise. Three is quite enough. And the first division championship the most important.

I would like to have a squad of 21 men, almost two teams, to select from according to the circumstances—to change them completely for the differing situations. This, to my mind, is the best way to tackle the job of going for the big trophies in such demanding contests as you can have at home and

Peter Thompson.

abroad.

With only a small selection of men, however good they are, they can be snuffed out as a force with just a few injuries.

Europe is an exciting proposition; it's a great experience for the players and a treat for the fans to see all the famous European players. It's uppermost in my plans.

When I look at my fine young team I can see one boy who is going to be the biggest name in Europe—and one of the world's best players.

John McLaughlin. In 1970–71, at only 18, he began to show all the promise of a genius. He has the brain of a brilliant footballer, he steals yards on speed, operates like a veteran of vast experience in midfield, lulls and tricks an opposition player into a helpless state. Mark his name well, McLaughlin.

Bobby Charlton and George Graham (Arsenal) in a heading duel at Highbury. Paddy Crerand looks on.

MORE ACTION FROM A CUP FINALIST

John Radford (Arsenal) puts one past Crystal Palace goalkeeper John Jackson.

The man worth £400,000

PIETRO ANASTASI

IN many ways I am something of an odd character in the terms of soccer in Italy. In the first place, I am a Sicilian, which may sound an unimportant fact to many people, but the truth is that players from the two big Italian islands—Sicily and Sardinia—have seldom made a mark in the big leagues. Both islands have good teams—Cagliari, of Sardinia were champions only recently, and Sicily has two top teams in Catania and Palermo—but these teams are staffed by players transferred from the mainland.

Then when I was just twenty I was sold to the most famous of all Italian clubs, Juventus, for a world record fee of well over £400,000. Work that out in Italian *lire* and it looks mighty impressive.

Finally, I am a striker, a rare breed in the world today which seems dominated by defensive and midfield players. And in Italian football to be a striker means that you are the man every team sets out to mark with incredible tightness.

I learned my soccer in Catania, where I was born, then moved North to Varese. The club was then in the Italian second division, but we achieved promotion at the end of that season and I found that I could score good goals even when we came up against some of the best club sides in Europe, playing in the Italian First Division, the *Serie A*. Then came the shock transfer. I was all set to join Inter Milan and in fact played in the Inter colours in the May of 1968 in a friendly game. But at half time in that game I was told that I had been transferred to Juventus. What a shock it was. But I'm happy now at Juve, the club with possibly the most glorious past in Italy.

Two months later and I helped Italy to win the European Nations Cup, winning my first cap in the first of the two finals against Yugoslavia, staying on to play in the replay a couple of days later. The fact that I scored Italy's second goal on that occasion indicated that I had really arrived, and since then I have played several more games for my country.

The big blow came in the summer of 1970. I was chosen to go to Mexico as a member of the Italian squad for the World Cup finals. A couple of hours before we were due to leave Rome, everything ready for our departure, I fell ill and was forced to go into hospital for an operation. No World Cup finals for me then. But I watched every game with fanatical concentration on the television and was delighted that Italy did so well. The way the players fought back against Germany was really incredible.

I have lost my place in the Italian team at the moment of writing, but I know that the Italian manager is a fair man and will call me up again as soon as he thinks I'm back into my best form.

The trouble is that in Italian football it is a hard job being one of the players who are pushed up front. Over the years I have managed to get away with some truly acrobatic stuff in front of goal. People often think that I do it to show off. I don't. The truth is that the marking in Italian league football is so tight, the number of players pulled back so vast, that you simply have to take each and every chance that comes your way.

There is a thrill about scoring goals *in rovesciata*—that is to say with an overhead bicycle kick. But often you simply don't have time to turn around and pick your spot. You simply must let fly at the first opportunity, and kicks such as these if they are on target are virtually unstoppable. Similarly with diving headers at the near post—you have to get down to them before the defence comes across to clear. Try and trap the ball, pull it back into a good shooting position and before you know where you are, the ball has been taken away from you.

Italy has, for the past ten or fifteen years, been the country where *catenaccio* has become most famous. *Catenaccio* is the system whereby teams em-

Asparukhov, Bulgaria.

ploy a sweeper to lie behind the defence and cover not merely the players in the centre, but also those at the sides. If for instance, you play through the middle, you will find yourself harrassed all the way by the centre-half, and even if you manage to get past him, the sweeper will be there waiting for you. If you move out to the wings to take advantage of the greater amounts of space out there, the sweeper may well be lying tight behind the fullback. It makes life very difficult for strikers.

They say that a sweeper is only employed by teams whose defenders are not good at man-to-man marking, but I know different. In Italy there is a tendency always to see games in terms not merely of overall play, but also of the various personal duels that are taking place on the field: wing against full-back, wing-half against inside-forward, centre-half against centre-forward. Sometimes the full-backs will lay off the attacking wingers, but the centre-half will never give his opponent the slightest bit of space in which to play. All the time he will be breathing down your neck, preventing you from finding the sort of time that can set you up for a shot at goal.

Little wonder then, that Italian strikers have to be good to earn their keep, and I think it's true to say that over the years Italy has produced as many good strikers as any other European country. You're good because you have to be good, and the money rewards are so great for winning even league games that the onus is always on you to score regularly. Strikers in Italy, as in other countries, are probably paid more than the other players, their valuation in transfer terms is higher.

Look at the table of scorers and the average scores in League games and you can see how hard it is to make your mark. Since the defensive network against you is so strong, since the midfield build-up is often very slow, it means that strikers have to move really fast to outwit the opposition. Playing for Varese in the second division and playing for Juventus in the first are very different things. In the lower grade of football you are up against players of inferior skills, so that no matter the number of players the opposition draw back in defence, you are always in with a good chance of scoring. Up

with the big teams and it's very different, particularly when you play for a top side such as Juventus. The teams that come to play us at Torino come looking for a draw. And when we go away and look as though we are going to play well, they tend to think negatively, to hold us to a draw on their home ground.

I was transferred to Juventus a few weeks after the club were eliminated by Benfica in the semi-finals of the European Cup. But this remains one of my greatest ambitions now. I would love nothing more than to help Juve to a championship win followed by a successful run in the European Cup. Juve are the Italian club with most supporters all over Europe and I'm sure that if we did well, we wouldn't want for terrific support wherever we played. In the British Isles, I know, there are thousands of Juventus fans, who wait expectantly every Monday for the Italian papers to reach them so that they can see how we have got on the previous day. And there are many fans also in countries such as Germany and Switzerland, France and Spain.

As it is the present Juventus side is one that is very young, with players who are going to be really good in two or three years time. I hope we come good soon, and I hope that I will still be there, back to my best form and able to take on, and beat, the best defences that are put up against us.

Howard Kendall pictured with Alan Ball and Archie Gemmill.

"IT'S ALL YOURS, BOBBY," SHOUTS GOAL ACE DENIS

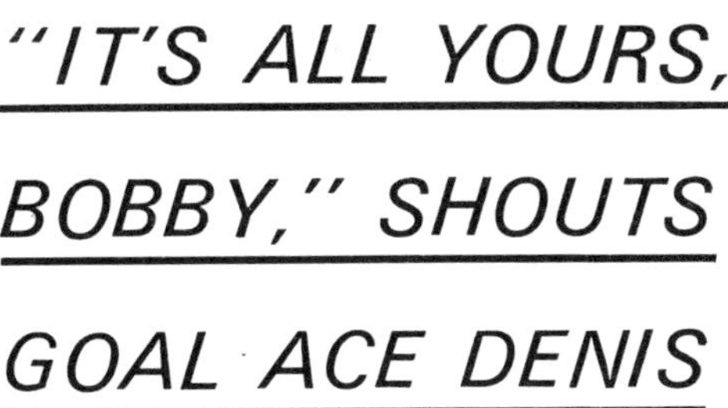

A typical piece of action from Bobby Charlton. Denis Law looks on as Bobby moves in to score, leaving the goalkeeper helpless.

GORDON BANKS..

Quote—from Gordon Banks's England team mate Bobby Charlton.

WHEN we saw him in training for the World Cup in Mexico he looked unbeatable. I've never seen him in greater condition or looking so indestructible. It was certainly no surprise to the England squad when he pulled off that incredible save against Pele.

"In fact, I think that some of the saves he made in training, with nobody around to see them but the squad and Sir Alf, were equally as good as that one which everybody in the world raves about.

"I am sure that any team, throughout the whole picture of soccer wherever it is played, would welcome him into its fold.

"I know that it is soul destroying to have to play against him. He is perfection in his job—and to get a shot past him is a major achievement.

"I remember Carlo Sartori playing for Manchester United at Stoke. He swung what was to be a short centre to another United forward in the middle. But he sliced it from the bye-line and the ball sailed in towards the Stoke goal. It surprised everybody but Banksie.

"Carlo was utterly defeated. He sat in the dressing room at half-time and said: 'How can you beat this man? What do you have to do?' He's not the first player to think like that.

"It was as if Carlo had given up. Anybody could have been forgiven for thinking he had beaten Gordon with such a surprise slice. And I suppose that a hundred other 'keepers would have been well-beaten.

"He didn't merely save it. It was the contemptuous way he did it that defeated us all.

"His title as the world number one is fair justification for his enormous skill. I've never seen a better 'keeper anywhere."

Goalkeeping according to the textbook. Gordon Banks (right) keeps his eyes on the ball. (Left) Toshack and Smith are in the action but Gordon, with the ball, is already looking for a chance to set up an attack.

BOBBY CHARLTON has told me that he has never seen me fitter or on greater form than I showed in Mexico during the World Cup contest in 1970.

I don't know about that but I must say I certainly felt fit and right on top form. I felt as good as I have ever done. Don't ask me why. It just seemed to work out that way.

I knew when I went to Mexico that the conditions there presented problems for a goalkeeper—the ball flew faster and did odd things in the air. It weaved and changed course as it came at you.

I had made up my mind that it would take some getting used to and I settled down to the idea that I would have to work especially hard to get my game right.

The pitches were bone hard and dusty, just the sort that a goalkeeper hates. The ball was lively and on the hard grounds goalkeeping was a painful occupation.

Every dive seemed to rattle my bones and bruise my hips. In the end I decided to train wearing knee-pads which afforded me some protection.

But even then I couldn't escape the more hurtful aspects of training; my feet became so blistered that I had to wear slippers. And one day one foot was so bad that I played with a football boot on one foot and a carpet slipper on the other. It was the only way I could get any relief from the monster sized blisters that had built up.

My other problem, the main one, was trying to get used to the speed of the ball and its puzzling antics in the Mexican atmosphere.

And in a bid to combat the problem I used to recruit the men with the hardest shots in the England squad, fellows like Geoff Hurst and Bobby Charlton, so they could put me through the hoop. They used to spend what time they could spare banging a ball at me from all angles and as hard as they could.

Eventually, facing men like these, I grew more confident in my ability to handle the ball. I began to get used to it; I got really sure of myself and, consequently, I felt that there was little I could not handle.

The ball, when it was shot hard and true, seemed

Bobby and Sir Alf Ramsey during training.

60

The penalty of a 'keeper's blunder

Jack Charlton did not give any second chances to Manchester City keeper Joe Corrigan. Joe dropped the ball in going to clear a corner and Jack hammered it in for a goal.

to come at me four or five yards quicker than it did at home in England. I couldn't rely too much on anticipation, the ball changed direction so much that to anticipate was to live dangerously. Instead I had to wait until the last minute, when the ball was right on me, before deciding how to deal with it.

It was the only way to be absolutely sure of getting to it. It made me look from time to time as if I was late in seeing a ball—but that wasn't the case. I just had to make certain that I didn't move too soon and that I wasn't left stranded with its last second movement in another direction.

I had noticed, too, on television that some Mexican goalkeepers wore leather gloves that had sort of pimples on the palms and on the finger ends.

I went out shopping for a pair and for the first time in my career I began to wear gloves on a dry day during a game. I found them a great help. Somehow the leather of the gloves and that of the ball seemed to have a sympathy and they stuck together like glue. It seemed, too, that if a ball was about to skid off the finger ends or break free the pimples on the gloves held it secure.

All these little things, the gloves, the endless hours of extra training I had put in and the confidence that emerged from the shooting practice given me by Bobby and Geoff, built up to a point where I felt really good. And I was pleased with the way I felt.

Some of the boys said I was as hard to beat in training as I was during a full-scale game with serious opposition. That was my plan. I trained just as if it was a match and everything depended on the saves I made.

It had to be that way. I had to shrug off the effects of the hard grounds, the whizzing ball, and go for everything that came at me as though my life depended on it.

Sir Alf Ramsey must have thought I was mad— I was always asking for extra training. But I knew it was paying off. I didn't know that a bad illness was shadowing me and was to cancel out all the hard work I had gone through.

When that dreadful stomach bug hit me and put me out of the game against West Germany I felt cheated and depressed.

I shared a room with Bobby Charlton and Keith

Newton and they both had a mild attack of the bug before the game—but they got over it. It hit me three times as hard and I had no chance despite the daily pills I had been taking to combat this sort of complaint.

Up to then I was really proud of my tan—it was about third best of the squad. But when I fell ill I went chalk white. I looked like Stan Laurel. All the energy and strength drained from me and I was helplessly weak.

When we got to Mexico City for the game, after a day long bus journey, I couldn't even carry my bags from the coach. Alex Stepney, my room-mate then, had to move them for me. And I went off to bed again.

The rest of the party went out for a training session but I stayed in bed with the doctor working on me trying to get me fit. For a while it seemed as if I would pull through in time for the game and I got up for a walk-round. Ten minutes later I was down again—and back into bed. The game, for me, was out of the question.

I know it has been suggested that I might have been nobbled, drugged, somehow but I discount that. I think it was something I ate or drank.

The effects of the illness lasted until a good few weeks after I had returned to England—and well into the new season of 1970. Tony Waddington, my boss at Stoke, had me isolated during games and I even had to bathe and shower alone, away from the rest of the lads.

And all my family had Ministry of Health checks in a bid to stave it off and sort out what it was all about. It took some time for it to finally disappear—but it left me weaker than I'd ever been before. So much for Mexico!

With my illness, the result against West Germany, the Bobby Moore bracelet affair and the World Cup without England, I lost my usual verve for the game at the start of the new season.

Usually with England the tours had been successful—except for the Little World Cup in 1966, when we finished joint bottom—and I came home feeling refreshed, revitalised and bursting to get into the new season. This time it was different.

Normally you want to get back onto the English grounds, to play in front of the crowds again, to feel the atmosphere and the tension. But this time I didn't. I wasn't stirred in the same way. And I felt that my play was affected by it.

This question of enthusiasm usually doesn't worry me at all; I don't have to manufacture it. It's there already. I'm so keen on the game, so anxious to get under way that my enthusiasm seems to be switched on without even thinking about it.

The day it isn't is the day I'll hang my boots up. My aim now is to get to Munich for the World Cup in 1974—and I know it depends on me entirely. I know I'll have to be on top form to realise that ambition.

The man on form will be the man to go when Sir Alf selects his squad. I'm going to try and make sure that I'm in the squad. I don't think my age then will make any difference at all if I'm playing well enough.

The minute I feel that I'm letting in soft goals or making mistakes that I would never have made before then I shall remove myself from the scene; I won't wait for somebody else to do it. But I won't drop down into the lower divisions—I hope to finish my career with Stoke in the first division.

I give myself a fairly stiff training schedule at Stoke. Long after the other boys have left I set to work on a series of exercises I have designed for my own job.

I work on keeping my stomach muscles toned up and my waist supple; then I do agility exercises, springing from the ball of my foot, running and leaping as high as I can.

I do precisely the same routines as an outfield player, the cross countries, the sprints and the lapping and ball work, but then I add to it with handling training. In the track work, twice a week, I'm never last. I'm always about the middle of the pack—but I can never win!

Training suits me. I like it. But you have to be honest with yourself—just as Bill Shankly says. If you slacken off you might get away with it for a few weeks, maybe even longer, but in the end it hits you. Suddenly you would find that something had gone wrong, you'd missed a ball, simply because you were not fit enough to leap after it or plunge down to it.

Soccer hot shot Peter Lorimer gives Blackpool new boy Neil Ramsbottom a taste of First Division shooting power.

The cumulative effects of skipping a training session, or not putting everything into it, of not having enough interest, would sure enough begin to show.

No professional footballer could afford to dodge the issue in his training. Not if he wants to be a force in the game.

I love to have a drink, for instance. But only in the early part of the week if we're not playing until Saturday. After Wednesday I don't bother. But on Saturday night I'll go out with my wife and sink a couple of pints and maybe a few Bacardi! But I don't get myself plastered. I know how to look after myself.

I think it does you no harm to have a few drinks now and again; it helps to relieve the tension you have been building up. I don't mind admitting the lads had a few after the World Cup final win in 1966. And we had a few more again when we were knocked out in 1970.

We didn't have anything to celebrate—but we drowned our sorrows on the 'plane home. It helped us forget and made us relax. It had been a long build up, an arduous one. We needed to let our hair down a little. . . And we did!

The UPS and DOWNS of Wyn The Leap

BY GEORGE!

Arsenal Go One Step Nearer that Wembley Triumph

Charlie George is the executioner again. His two-goal tally (top and middle) in a night replay at Maine-road put Manchester City out of the 1970–71 FA Cup. But (below) City's Colin Bell strikes back to floor Arsenal keeper Bob Wilson with his shooting skill.

''Newcastle United have been far too long out of the limelight in the hunt for home trophies. The fans in the great North-East soccer field deserve success and we aim to give it to them.''

Newcastle —a team on the fringe

TRADITION, like the chill wind that blows history through St. James' Park, has kept Newcastle United alert to the constant needs of winning top honours and alive to the problems of giving the fans success.

Europe beckoned us and in season 1968–69 we, the comparative newcomers to continental competition, scooped up the major prize of the Fairs Cup trophy, following in the footsteps of Leeds United and preceding Arsenal who clinched it the following year.

Newcastle United have appeared ten times in the FA Cup Final, a record we share with West Brom, and we have taken the Cup to Tyneside half a dozen times, the last being in 1955.

So it's in the club's lifestream to have Cup success. Though we managed to bring home the Fairs Cup trophy by beating Ujpest Dosza, the team that had brushed aside Leeds United, we had to do it abroad.

It would have given us tremendous satisfaction if we could have completed the second leg, and the win, at Newcastle in front of our own crowd. However, as it turned out, we couldn't have had a better reception.

It seemed that the whole place had turned out to welcome us home; in fact many of the big firms had given their men half a day off to greet us. It was just like the good old days with a trophy being paraded for the fanatical North-Eastern fans. I think it took all the players back to the time when famous players like Jackie Milburn, Alf McMichael and our boss, Joe Harvey, were bringing great honour to Tyneside.

It was even more satisfying to us, the players, because we had started underdogs, written off by the so-called experts.

They gave us no chance at all against the team that had wiped the mighty Leeds United out of the trophy and, it seemed to everybody but us, the final was a cut and dried affair. But we played magnificently and flattened them.

The following year I thought we were on the way to bringing home the trophy once more—but Anderlecht, the team that finally lost to Arsenal in the final, knocked us out. The two legs gave us a three–three draw but they went through on away goals.

There were more than 60,000 fans crammed into St. James' Park that night and sadly we had to fail them. We'd gone down 2–0 in Belgium and hit them 3–1 at home . . . but that single away goal clinched

it for them.

Even after those ups-and-downs in the Fairs contest I think that if you asked all the Newcastle United fans whether they'd rather have the league or a cup they'd be split down the middle. There's nothing like a cup final win, in any competition, Europe or domestic, to excite the fans. There is something special, particularly in the FA Cup, which seems to generate tremendous interest.

Nowhere in the world, certainly nowhere that I have been, gets greater feeling for a cup than the Newcastle crowd; it's in their blood through the fine traditions of the club's Wembley successes.

It's always satisfying for the professional to be in a side that wins the league, the long drawn out effort and the consistency needed give him great pleasure when it's all over. The quick death of cup soccer stirs him, of course, but it seems to stir the fans into a fever that the league only gets in the last few games when it's almost all over and done with.

It's probably that the whole character of the North East, tough and rugged and brought up on soccer excitement, lends itself to football atmosphere.

We seem to be able to gobble up the London clubs, for instance. The journey up there must seem like a ride into another continent, it's so far. And, when they get to St. James' Park, that chill wind is always shrieking across the grass, it's usually freezing cold, damp and dismal. There's no built up stand area to block the wind; it swirls almost incessantly.

The toss is always a good thing to win at Newcastle. It's a habit I have now of glancing up at which way the flags are fluttering when the referee whistles the skippers up to the middle. You can almost always guarantee getting a good stiff breeze in your favour if you win the toss—the other side is left to plough against it through the whole of the first half.

We have adapted our play to suit the conditions that prevail at Newcastle and it's small wonder that few clubs enjoy playing us up there. Few goalkeepers, who know the problems, ever throw a ball clear. It will most probably come roaring back at them,

Wyn Davies.

carried on the wind.

When we started into Europe I think few clubs abroad knew who we were; some did not even know where Newcastle was and our players, aside from the internationals in the side, were unknown outside England. But they know us now—we made them with our play and our determination.

It didn't hurt us; we didn't worry that other clubs like Manchester United, Spurs and Leeds were better known. In fact we rather preferred to be the underdogs. That way nobody expected anything special from us and were surprised when they got it.

It makes a team fight harder if they have been virtually written off into second place of two starters; favourites tend to be a little too complacent.

When we played Inter-Milan in the fabulous

71

Bryan 'Pop' Robson, sold to West Ham United, late in the 1970/71 season is pictured here in action in his Newcastle United days.

San Siro only a handful of spectators turned up.

The stadium was more like a morgue and it affected the Italians. I suppose the fans, again, had shrugged us off as no-hopers who wouldn't give their favourites much of a challenge so they didn't bother to turn up.

It created an awful lethargy among the Inter-Milan side; their confidence was doused and they began to play a cat-and-mouse game instead of a full-blooded competition. I was amazed—and so were they when Wyn Davies finally shattered all that remained of their ego with a headed goal that made him the talk of Italy.

I don't know just how widely known Wyn was before that goal but certainly afterwards his name was one to be feared.

I don't think that Wyn is the finest header of a ball, but I don't think anybody in the world gets as high to meet it as he does. The chances he lays off for others are endless.

Once, when we were training, I remember throwing a ball to him. It seemed high to me—but he got up to it. I did it again, and again, until the ball, it seemed to me, was just a dot in the sky. But everytime up went Wyn and got his head to it. Imagine having to face a man like that, and one who is brave enough to go in whatever the circumstances. No wonder the Europeans have a great regard for his ability. They don't have anybody to match his skill and talent for leaping.

The difficulty about playing for a club like Newcastle, which is not as 'fashionable' as teams like Manchester United, Liverpool and, say, Arsenal and Leeds, is that it is difficult to earn recognition as a good candidate to represent your country's national side.

And, here, the value of playing in Europe and being noticed comes across.

I had gained an under-23 cap for Scotland and then a full cap for Scotland against Holland and everything on the international front seemed to be going well for me. Suddenly my fortunes changed— I suffered a cartilage problem which put me out of the running. That, I was sure, was that and I cursed my luck at not being in a more 'fashionable' side.

However, when we won the Fairs Cup, we played Rangers in the semi-final which was televised. I had a good game and, of course, with the match being on television and seen by so many influential people in Scotland I got myself back into their eye as a possible for Scotland again.

This fact, and that we were so successful in Europe helped me personally no end—it put me right back in the reckonings.

Normally, to stand any chance of getting into the national side, a player has to be in the limelight, with a top flight club that is being successful most of the time. The men with the more 'fashionable' sides and those with the successful teams always get first bite of the cherry when it comes to being noticed by the selectors.

There are very many good players who, quite simply, have not had the chance to prove themselves as internationals because they are out of the limelight.

Look at Archie Gemmil. He was almost hidden away until Derby County let him play in the Ibrox testimonial match in Glasgow. He had such a great game, with so many leading lights of Scottish soccer watching him, that he was drafted straight into the side to meet Belgium a week later. He might have gone for months, years, without getting his due recognition.

Without our success in Europe, and that televised Rangers game, the same thing could well have happened to me.

Now we at Newcastle United are on the fringe of being 'fashionable' and, with a little more luck, we hope to make the complete breakthrough and win something really big in 1971–72. I hope it's the league. The fans, or half of them at least, would like it to be the FA Cup. Either way it's a gateway to Europe again—and that's where we deserve to be. If only for the sake of all those great Tyneside fans.

I am so determined to put everything into my soccer, and win something again, that I've put off going into business.

I want to be able to concentrate fully on soccer. I reckon the three best years of my career are now stretching out in front of me.

Just watch Newcastle go in Europe! We have had the taste and we liked it. Now we want a bigger bite.

Martin Chivers dishing it out and Spurs taking it. .

cheeky goal from Manchester United's George Best, off the picture.

TENSION
at the big games

Best, Peters and Francis Burns at a United versus Spurs game at Old Trafford.

Colchester's Dave Simmons and Norman Hunter, of Leeds United in a Cup-tie confrontation.

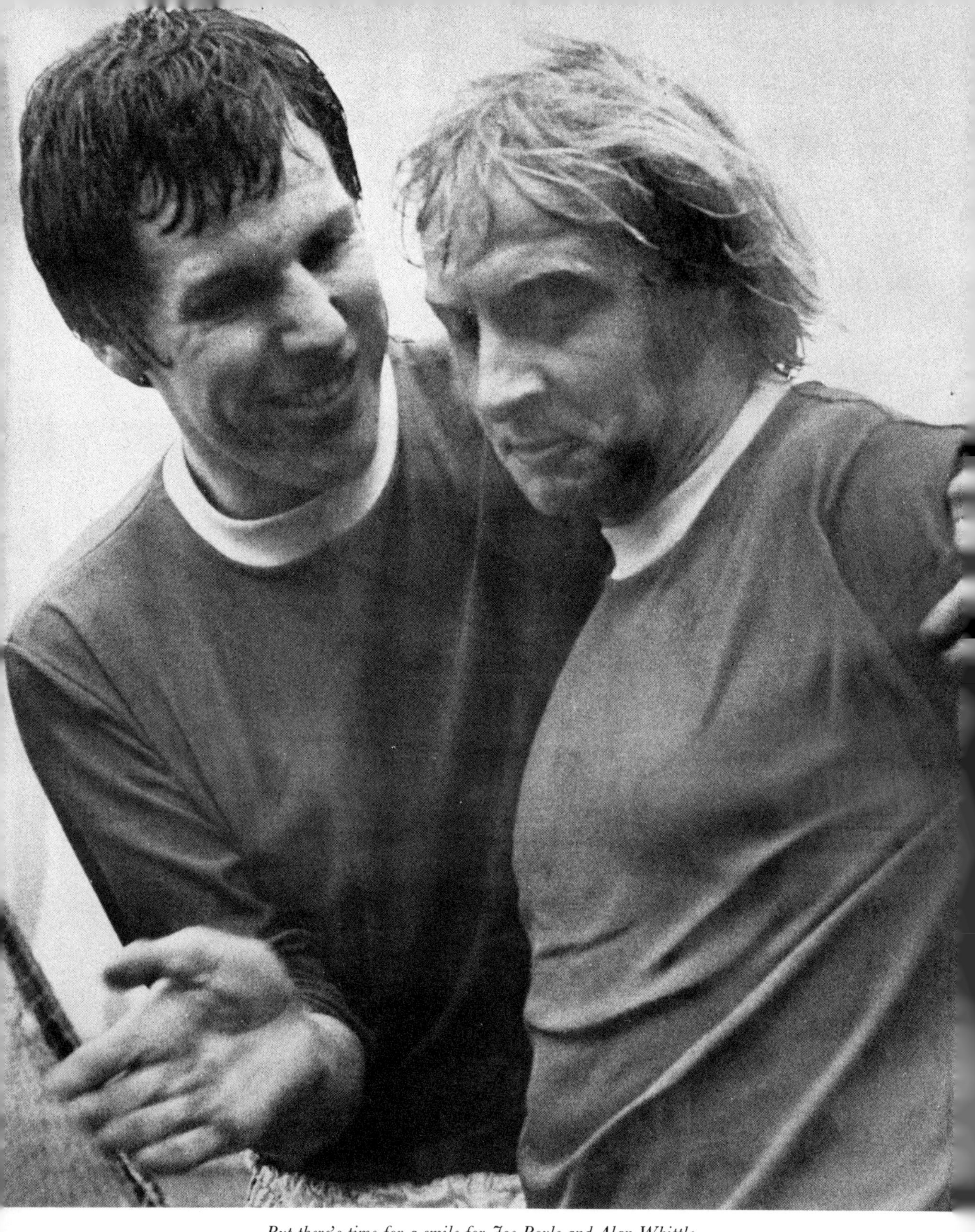

But there's time for a smile for Joe Royle and Alan Whittle. . .

. . . and Alan's double, Denis Law shown here with Stoke City's Harry Burrows.

WING TROUBLE FOR PALACE

Willie Morgan, Manchester United's £100,000 winger takes on Steve Kember of Crystal Palace.

George Best, hair flying, races against Palace defender Blyth.

THE CAPTAINS:
North and South

Famous team leaders pictured in pairs. Below; Bobby Charlton, of Manchester United, and his London counterpart Chelsea's Ron Harris. Right; Alan Ball, Everton and Alan Mullery, Spurs.

The Team that came back from beyond

By FRANK McLINTOCK

IT was a spring night in Brussels and I was convinced that the jinx which seems to shadow me to all big occasion matches had struck again.

There were 37,000 fans watching Anderlecht and Arsenal trying to break each other's grip on the first leg of the Fairs Cup final.

We were playing well, I thought, moving the ball round easily and not too worried about Anderlecht's threat when they suddenly hit us. Almost before we realised they had gone into a three goal lead.

It was as if Anderlecht were writing another chapter into my own personal bad luck story. Four times, with Leicester City and Arsenal, I had been on the losing side in FA and League Cup finals.

Now it seemed that it was all happening again; to top it all I had my work cut out trying to cope in a tremendous tussle with Anderlecht's centre-forward, Mulder, who was most certainly the best I have ever played against.

He was really skilful; he could screen a ball beautifully and with such a guard that it was difficult to get it off him. He could move with it, lay it off and shoot with deadly power and accuracy. He was a big man with plenty of weight to back up his determination and he had this knack of running right at you at full speed and then swerving away, right or left, at the last second.

With van Himst, the inside left, supporting him so well Mulder scored two. The inside right, Devrindt, scored the other and we hadn't even managed to find our way to goal.

I couldn't begin to explain how downhearted I felt; I began to believe that I really did have a jinx. And I groaned to myself: "Well, I've done it again!"

Up to this final, after all the other disappointments, I tried to put it to the back of my mind. I persuaded myself that if I kept playing well every-

Arsenal are defending in depth, and directing their every move is skipper Frank *McLintock*, Footballer of the Year, FA Cup winning skipper, league championship medal winner and Scottish international.

The two Johns, Sammels and Radford, surround a Liverpool player.

George Armstrong.

Peter Storey, Bob McNab and Peter Simpson break up a Manchester City raid.

thing would turn out okay and I would master this hoodoo and would be able to put it behind me. I thought I must keep pegging away and everything would turn out all right in the end.

After a long professional career in soccer all I had to show for it in terms of prizes was a gold medal I had won with Leicester reserves when we finished champions in the London Combination!

I must say this for the Arsenal boys—they didn't know how to quit. We all knew that we had a chance of putting the club's name back onto the soccer map, even though we were three goals down. And traditions are important to Arsenal.

In the last few minutes Ray Kennedy came on as substitute and managed, at last, to find a fault in Anderlecht's defence and score. It really was a golden goal; it counted double and it put us right back into the game for the second leg at Highbury.

In London we faced the dilemma of having to go out to attack and score—but not let them score. It's history now, but we managed it and in front of nearly 52,000 spectators we knocked in three more and won one of Europe's top prizes.

I felt it was ironical that having failed to win anything in the domestic competitions I should manage to be on the winning side in one of soccer's toughest contests.

I don't mind admitting now that I cried like a baby that night. The scene was altogether too much.

I remember thinking that April 28, 1970, would always live in my memory. When I picked up the cup I felt a great surge of pride; I tried to run with it around the stadium but it was impossible. The whole pitch was black with people, everybody was milling round slapping backs, trying to touch the cup, pushing and shoving and fighting to get near.

It was incredible and there had been nothing like it at Highbury for years; you could feel the atmosphere, feel the pride of the players that they'd won something important for Arsenal. I had to be rescued by the police after only about fifty yards of running with the Fairs Cup—I was bruised more by the crowd than I had been in both the games. But it didn't matter to me, I was overjoyed.

We'd been a bit too cocky in Brussels. We thought we didn't have to do anything to win and we had been strolling round, playing the ball probably too loosely thinking "they'll never score". When they did we thought that they wouldn't be able to do it again—but they did, of course, twice. We didn't make the same mistake at Highbury.

There can be no doubt that European soccer is a tremendous experience, not only for the players but for the fans, too.

They can see teams that have been only names to them; they can see, and enjoy, the different types of skills of top European players who have only been figures on a television screen to them.

To play in any European competitions is thrilling for the players; and it is certainly a bonus, a great fillip to spectators. It was like the beginning of a great revival for us at Arsenal when we won the cup.

Mick Jones, the man who spearheaded Leeds United in their battle with Arsenal for the first division crown.

We've hardly looked back since.

We had not had a great deal of experience of European competitions at Arsenal. We'd played friendlies, of course, but it's not the same as fierce competition for a top award.

But, on the way to the final, we really began to believe we had made a great breakthrough when we beat Sporting Lisbon, a team with a superb reputation abroad.

In Lisbon we held them 0–0, and when they visited Highbury we whacked them 3–0 with goals from John Radford and George Graham who scored two. I think then that we really began to believe in ourselves as good competition for any of the sides in the hunt for the cup.

The fact that I managed to beat my own jinx gave me a great deal of personal satisfaction; this, allied to a magnificent team show, ensured my appetite for leading Arsenal to further honours, not only in Europe, of course, but at home, too.

I think that Arsenal have greater potential now than they have had for years. It is a great side in prospect; there is a depth of reserve strength, European experience to help, a great tradition to uphold and, most important, a belief that we can do what we set out to do.

It seems to me that with an outfit like Arsenal's around me I might yet still manage to be on a winning side in a Cup Final. Who knows? It could be fifth time lucky for me.

Anyway, the boys at Highbury don't call me a jinx any longer. It seems as if I have put that reputation behind me.

When Arsenal emerge to real greatness—and I promise you it will happen as a natural development in the next five years—then I think the fans will see, too, the re-emergence of Peter Marinello.

It cost the club £100,000 to sign him and he got off to a disappointing start. Too many people expected too much from him too soon—but the club has been working on him, building up his strength and improving his play to add to all his natural ability.

When he first arrived from Scotland a lot of the players, and a good many spectators, took the mickey out of him. He was a victim, I suppose, of

Eusebio.

the build-up he was given. He was the new "George Best" and sponsors were crowding in on him to get him signed up and commercialised. London was ready then for its own "George Best" and saw Peter as the player ready made for the glamour treatment.

The poor boy never got a chance to settle in and, quite naturally, his play suffered. But you watch this next few years; he, like Arsenal, will be a force to be reckoned with.

The players called him Catweazle—"Cat" for short. And it's a name that's stuck. Towards the end of February, 1971, they were saying that the "Cat" was playing really well in the reserves and was hunting for a first-team place.

It's a tribute to his own character that he has survived it all and has broken through as a player whose potential will be an asset to Arsenal. Now it's up to the rest of the regular forwards at Highbury to look out for their jobs because the way he is going Peter is going to be a serious threat.

On Your Marks..

Ready, steady go for Bobby Charlton against the best of Stoke's sprinters.

SUMMER STRIPPER

Denis Law, Manchester United's goal scoring genius who usually makes it hot for others finds things getting a bit warm. But quick thinking Denis showed what he is made of in dealing with this situation in a Watney Cup tie at Reading.

WINTER WALLOWERS

Mudbath football for big rivals Manchester United and Manchester City. Taking the treatment in this particular action are Tony Dunne (United) Ian Bowyer (City, now with Orient) Paul Edwards and David Sadler (United).

The Club Championship Squabbles

By FRANZ HASIL

IN the early summer of 1970 Feyenoord won the European Cup. The Cup has been played for and won again since then, but that victory remains fresh in the minds of many people who have never had any contact with Dutch football.

It remains vividly in the minds of many Italians. For years they have played to *catenaccio* systems in Italy, pulling wingers back, employing a sweeper. And in doing so, Italian club football has too often seemed ultra-defensive and unentertaining to watch. We played *catenaccio* in our game against Celtic, but the game we played bore no comparison to that normally played in Italy. It was a fine example of the saying that any soccer system is only as good as the players who play it. And most important we used the system as a method of attack, rather than one of defence.

The manager of Feyenoord, Ernst Happel, is an Austrian, like myself. But it is more than merely national ties that makes me admire him so much. Throughout his career he has developed a talent for predicting the outcome of various games, rather in the same way that Helenio Herrera did in his days with Inter Milan. From the start of the European Cup campaign the manager was confident that we would do well, even when we were drawn to meet the holders in the early rounds—

Hasil.

David Hay.

obby Charlton with Estudiantes star Pachame and one of Bobby's dazzling daughters.

A.C. Milan. But Mr. Happel came up with a scheme to defeat Milan and was proved right. It is true that at the time the Italian team were involved in games against the South Americans, Estudiantes. But throughout the competition, after we had beaten them, the Milan players remained convinced that we would do well, even when the limelight was thrown over other teams in the competition, such as Celtic and Leeds United.

The manager is one of the best tacticians in the modern game, with a keen eye for the merits and defects of every player he sees. He watched Milan play before we were due to meet them, and came up with the right formula. And he watched Celtic play and came up with the prediction that, although Celtic were unquestionably a very good side, they could be beaten.

That European Cup final was fascinating from both points of view—in general terms and from my own angle. Mr. Happel decided that the best method of countering Celtic's style of play—which is basically 4-2-4, with four good runners up front and two men in midfield—was to play *catenaccio*. But this was to be not merely a defensive system, it was also to be the springboard for quick breaks out of defence, running straight into the Celtic midfield, where the Scots team was short in numbers.

It was partly deception on Mr. Happel's part. Several weeks before the European Cup final, the Celtic manager had travelled over to Holland to watch us play. We threw away a 3-1 lead, our defence had an unhappy time, and Jock Stein must have gone home to Scotland convinced that a player such as the sinuous Jimmy Johnstone would be able to run rings around our defence. Certainly in the two semi-final ties he turned on excellent performances.

In Milan however, Johnstone had an unhappy match, a fact compounded by the way in which we detailed two men to mark him out of the game. The skipper of our team, Israel, fell back to become sweeper, another player, Jansen, normally a mid-field man, came back to play in the back four. This meant that we had weight in numbers at the back, but that the auxiliary players who had been drafted in were not merely defenders, but midfield men, who could pass the ball accurately and break out of defensive positions with good ball control and an eye for openings.

Celtic were stretched all over the field, forced to push men forward so that their midfield and defence became weak. This left Ove Kindvall up front alone to take whatever chances came his way, and the way in which he scored our second goal in extra time was magnificent.

From a personal point of view I was highly pleased with my own performance. First there is the point that although I am Austrian I play for a Dutch team—this means that I am usually out in the cold as far as international games are concerned, able to play for my country usually when I am not involved in club football with Feyenoord. Then there is the fact that I had a very enjoyable evening in Milan against Celtic. I hit the bar once, the post once, missed both by a whisker on other occasions and was able to take advantage of Celtic's weakness in midfield to move forward myself as well as setting up chances for the front-runner.

There is nothing a midfield player likes more than the chance to move into attacking positions himself. Of course it is always satisfying when your passes are perceptive and accurate and cut right through an opposing defence. But to go up and have an attempt at scoring yourself makes you feel part of the most exciting aspect of the game. For this reason the game against Celtic was one of the most enjoyable I have ever played.

But on from Celtic to Estudiantes. And few people blamed our club when it seemed that we might not bother to play against the champions of South America. In the previous three years the games between the European Cup holders and the South American teams had degenerated into the most incredible affairs. Celtic were stoned and spat at; Manchester United were intimidated at all points and Milan were brutalised in the second leg. In the end we played and were surprised. But only temporarily.

The first game, played in Buenos Aires, made the Devil seem as though he was on holiday. Estudiantes took a quick two-goal lead, never put a foot wrong and seemed to be coasting to an easy victory when we struck back with two goals from Ove Kindvall and Van Hanegem. But even with the scores level the Argentinians played a clean game. Neither we—nor the millions watching the match in Holland on television—could believe our eyes. It was as though we had come for a violent election meeting and found ourselves discussing topics quietly and fairly.

But Estudiantes reverted to their normal be-haviour in the second leg, back in Rotterdam. There, 67,000 people turned up for the game, cheering us on wildly, all witnesses to the way in which Estudi-antes can play. They aren't a very good side at all,

Wyn Davies kicks up the dust against Wolves.

in fact they are poor. They have one or two good players, but not enough, and on the whole their tactics are simple. They merely try to drive the opposing side off the field by fouling them, spitting at them, tripping and kicking.

In the first game I found that Estudiantes had no way of countering quick attacks. Like many Latin teams they play shuffle-ball, walking around at a slow pace, building up moves with care, trying to strike quickly when they get close to goal. Several times I had run the ball at the defence fast, giving them no time to get into position. But in the return match such tactics were a waste of time. From the first whistle the South Americans showed their true colours by body-checking and tripping any player who seemed to be in a dangerous position. And they went really mad when we scored our goal in the second half. The reason for their rage was hard to comprehend. It was scored by a young player who had never before played a full game for Feyenoord, Joop Van Deale. But the Estudiantes complaints seemed to centre around the fact that Joop plays in spectacles! And soon after one of their players took Joop out of the game by breaking his spectacles in two.

The last twenty minutes of the game were fearful, with the South Americans running around like mad dogs. But we had won. We had added another important cup to our collection. We had become the first Dutch club to win the European trophy and had helped our fans to feel proud in the face of all the triumphs piled on recently by Ajax of Amsterdam.

But little wonder when, after we had defeated Estudiantes, our manager informed the press of his secret. He had decided during the second of our matches against the South Americans, and in view of their vile play, that if a third match were necessary to decide the champions of the cup, Feyenoord wouldn't play. Who can blame him when football is reduced in this manner to the sort of thing that is more appropriate on a battlefield?

HANDCLAPS . . . *Leeds United players line up to make an applauding guard of honour for Bobby Charlton after he had gained his 100th international cap for England.*

FOR 100 CAPS

And here's Bobby sitting amid them all at his home in Cheshire's stockbroker belt. Said Bobby: "A century of caps for England is an unbelievable honour."

THE MEN FOR MUNICH 1974?

Peter Shilton of Leicester City and England.

Steve Kindon

Brian Kidd

Alan Hudson : Emlyn Hughes

Henry Newton : Colin Bell

A little tiddler in a big soccer pool...

By SHAY BRENNAN

Shay Brennan, former Manchester United fullback star, who tasted the triumphs in Europe with a big time team tells what it's like to be boss of tiddler club Waterford.

GOING into Europe with my club Waterford is a much different proposition than it was travelling the same football path with Manchester United.

Nobody's heard of Waterford. Who hasn't heard of Manchester United?

Three times we have been the champions of the Republic of Ireland in the last four years and that has qualified us for the European Cup alongside big names like Celtic, Real Madrid, Benfica, Manchester United and Ajax, the most famous names in soccer.

The furthest we ever got in the competition was into the second round after beating Northern Irish champions Glentoran in 1970—then we were paired with Celtic! I ask you—what chance did we have?

I had just taken over at Waterford on a three year contract when the European Cup draw was to be made in Amsterdam; and off I went on my first official trip for the club.

With Manchester United, as a player, I simply accepted what the club organised for me as a member of the unit. With Waterford, as the boss, I was more deeply involved. I was the one who had to do the organising—and the worrying! What a totally different world it had suddenly become!

I had never even given the slightest thought to being a manager before I was approached by Waterford. In fact, Jimmy Melia wanted me to extend my playing days at Aldershot and Alan Ball, Preston's new boss, asked me to join him when my career was ending at Old Trafford.

After all the glory with United, the magnificent treatment we got wherever we went in the world, the glamour of the club, the famous players and, of course the boss, Sir Matt Busby, I didn't want to become a soccer drop-out stepping into the shadows of the lower leagues when I had tasted the best in football life.

But what else was there for me? I had not bothered

Happy days in Europe with Bobby Charlton and Nobby Stiles.

Great moments a
home with the lad
parading the Leagu
Championship Cu
at Old Trafford.

Another happy moment in Europe, this time with Paddy Crerand, Harry Gregg and Bobby in Austria.

to take a coaching course and the idea of being a boss never cropped up. Then, right out of the blue, the Waterford contract came up. . .

I helped United to a 1–0 win over Ipswich in the FA Cup then put my mind to the idea of being manager of Ireland's most successful club.

When we had whacked Glentoran and had, for the first time in our history, got into the second-round of a top international tournament where prestige was heightened the atmosphere in the town was fantastic.

We were going into the hat with frightening names like Celtic, Everton, Red Star Belgrade, Ajax, the holders, Feyenoord, Sporting Lisbon and Atletico Madrid.

My head was spinning at the prospects when I climbed aboard the jet for the flight to Amsterdam for the draw.

Somebody asked: "Which club would you like to draw?" And I replied: "The smallest." And I was told: "Well, you can't draw yourselves YOU are the smallest . . . Waterford!"

"All right," I said, "we'll have the biggest. Celtic. that'll do for us."

When the draw was made Waterford was the first name to emerge and then we all held our breath. Who was it going to be? Borussia Munchen-Gladbach? Panathinaikos in Athens?

" . . . will play Celtic," intoned the official who made the draw.

I couldn't believe my ears. Celtic. Just what we wanted. We didn't wait for the rest of the draw we simply rushed off to the bar to celebrate. And it was an extremely merry Shay Brennan, one of the soccer's newest, and certainly happiest, managers who staggered aboard the 'plane for the journey back home.

We didn't kid ourselves that we would beat Celtic—but stranger things have happened. Look at Norwich and Manchester United, Leeds and Colchester.

What we did know was that it was a winner in another way. A money spinner for us. Unlike the year before when we played a Turkish team, Galatasaray, and went down 2–0 in the first leg over there, and lost 3–2 in front of 12,000 fans in Waterford. That draw was a financial disaster for the club and we lost something like £3,000.

We knew we would never cram all the people who wanted to see this game into our tiny ground so we moved the game up to Dublin's Lansdowne Road.

Not since we had been drawn against Manchester United in the first round European Cup in the 1968–69 season had so much excitement been generated around Waterford.

United had won both legs. 3–1 and 7–1—but, again, the real winner, so far as Waterford was concerned, was the bank balance.

We planned and re-planned, still hoping for the miracle of a win in the first leg, but Celtic hit us with everything they had in their arsenal. They did us the honour of really trying—and they scored straight from our kick-off. Ten minutes later they had made it two and we were on the downward run.

They finished 7–0 winners—but, even now, I don't think they were that much better than we were and we played some good football. Celtic, however, were too powerful, and too experienced for us.

At Parkhead we had heard that Jock Stein was going to draft in one or two reserves but he didn't and, despite the massive lead his side had, they still fielded a full strength team.

We played superbly—and managed to earn a 2–0 lead. It looked to me as if we might do it, as if we might at least beat them in front of their own fans. But they hit back to take a 3–2 final lead.

People in Scotland had been talking of a record scoring total in the European Cup and thinking that Celtic might pop in another seven—but we had other plans and I think we emerged with honour. And certainly with around £20,000.

With only seven full-time professionals and the rest of the staff made up of amateurs and part-time professionals a pay out of that size was a great reward for the club.

We only just missed the championship again in 1970/71, which would have been a record number of successive wins of the title, but I don't think that Europe is too much of a treat for a club of our size. Of course we would have gone into the competition and would have done our best—but, unless we got a good draw, it could be financially problematical for us again.

Ideally, Europe ends for us in Britain. With the chance of getting a big club like Manchester United, Everton, Leeds or Arsenal or Celtic as a draw all aspects of our situation are covered.

We are guaranteed a good pay out, a good crowd, certainly at home, and a drastic reduction in travelling expenses.

It won't stop me aiming for Europe's top contests—but we at Waterford, with our limited resources, must never delude ourselves that we can live the international big-time on a shoe-string budget in far off places like Turkey and Russia with little hope of any return for our effort.

SOCCER IN THE BALANCE

EUROPE'S top soccer competition, the Champions' Cup, could be completely dominated this season by a British club with one of the finest backgrounds of tradition in the whole football spectrum.

Arsenal, only the second team to complete the league championship and FA Cup double this century, will carry England's hopes into Europe's soccer battlefields after one of the most exciting finishes to the championship in the history of the game.

Few sides, with the possible exception of Leeds United, are as well equipped as the determined Londoners to carry off the European Cup trophy. And certainly there are few in Europe to match their all-round qualities.

"They are a team with great character and tremendous depth of strength," says their manager, Bertie Mee.

He added: "Look at the way they came back in the Cup Final. They were tremendous. They showed fight and an ability to pick themselves up from the disappointment of being a goal behind."

"A fine side," conceded Leeds United's boss, Don Revie, after his side had been pipped by Arsenal for a place in the European Cup.

Arsenal skipper Frank McLintock, who finally laid his Wembley jinx at the fifth attempt, told me after his side's double achievement: "We are ready and equipped to take on the best on the continent. And I am convinced we can do well.

"This side of ours can only get better. In two years' time, given normal luck and following the

North or South for the titles? TED MACAULEY looks at the evidence of the results in this year's Cup and League games

110

Steve Perryman and Alan Ball in close contact.

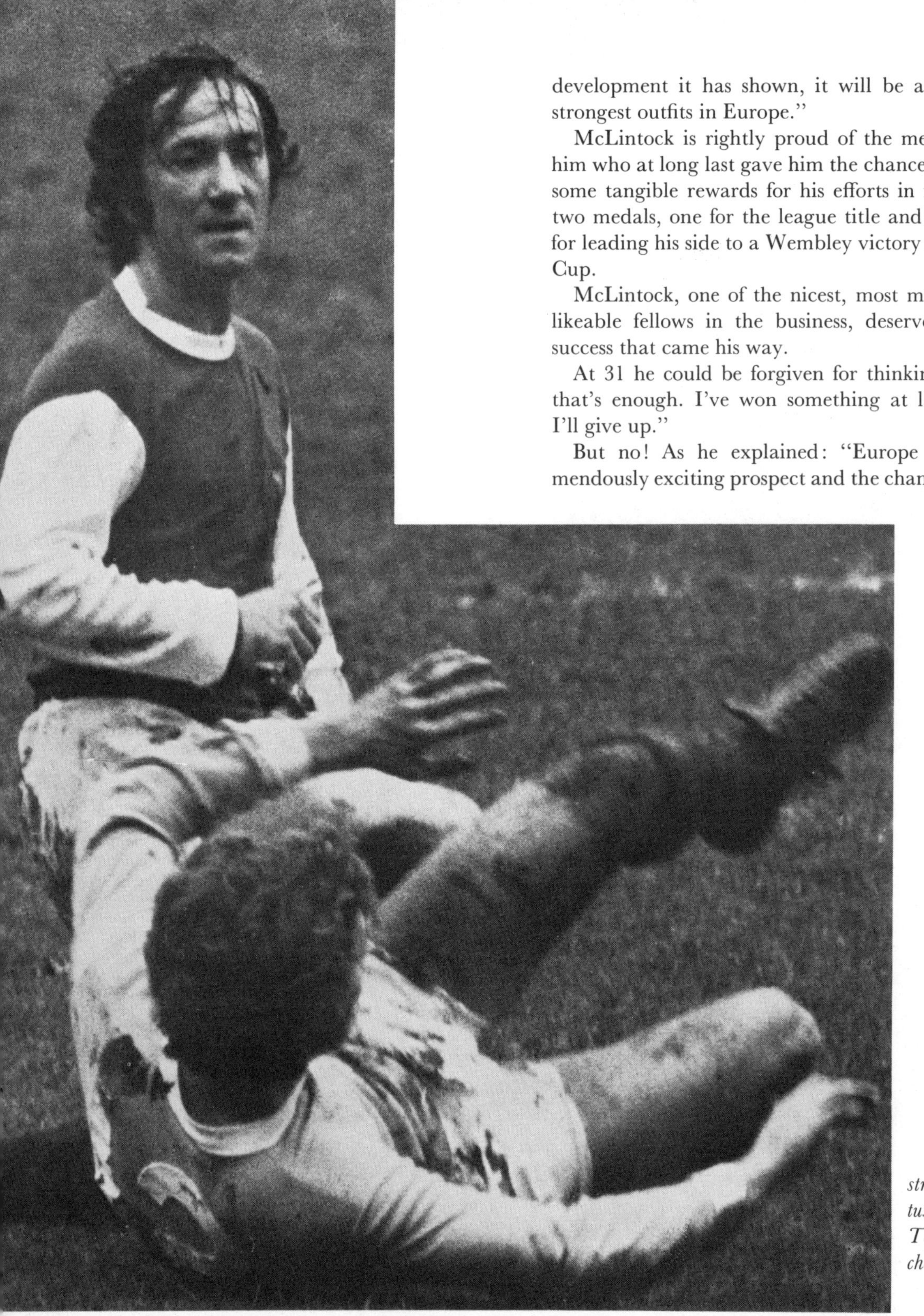

development it has shown, it will be among the strongest outfits in Europe.''

McLintock is rightly proud of the men around him who at long last gave him the chance to collect some tangible rewards for his efforts in football—two medals, one for the league title and the other for leading his side to a Wembley victory in the FA Cup.

McLintock, one of the nicest, most modest and likeable fellows in the business, deserves all the success that came his way.

At 31 he could be forgiven for thinking: "well, that's enough. I've won something at last. Now, I'll give up."

But no! As he explained: "Europe is a tremendously exciting prospect and the chance to take

Geordie Armstrong, of Arsenal tussles with Tony Towers, of Manchester City.

A CHARLTON RIGHT AND LEFT...

Alan Gilzean and Martin Chivers salute a Spurs goal.

on the best there is over there is as thrilling a thought as you could imagine. I'm looking forward to it.

"Arsenal has a great tradition to preserve. I am conscious of it and so are the rest of the boys. To bring the European Cup home to London would be the highpoint of my career. And we'll certainly be trying next year."

The emergence of Arsenal as a force in British football has adequately shown that the balance of power in soccer is being tilted from its almost permanent position in the North to a new level in the South.

They saw off Leeds in the league, Liverpool in the Cup final, and on the way knocked England's top pot hunters, Manchester City, aside with ridiculous ease. Behind them Tottenham Hotspur and Chelsea both showed a respectability in the league and a

promise that will almost certainly lift them even higher up the first division next season.

Chelsea flagged only because of a series of dreadful injuries and the suspension of Peter Osgood; Spurs, with so much talent, began to hit a smooth patch.

Who can deny that they will be a force to be reckoned with in this coming season? Martin Peters, after a shaky start, found his feet with them. Martin Chivers, boosted by Sir Alf Ramsey's recognition of his England potential, is another player who blossomed to greatness.

And now, with the £190,000 Ralph Coates bringing strength and stamina to the right flank, Spurs must surely be the most complete outfit in the land.

I put money on Arsenal in season 1970-71—and it paid off; I fancied them for the Cup long before

No surrender
here from
Hull City's
Ken Wagstaff
...but his club
still didn't make
it into the
first division

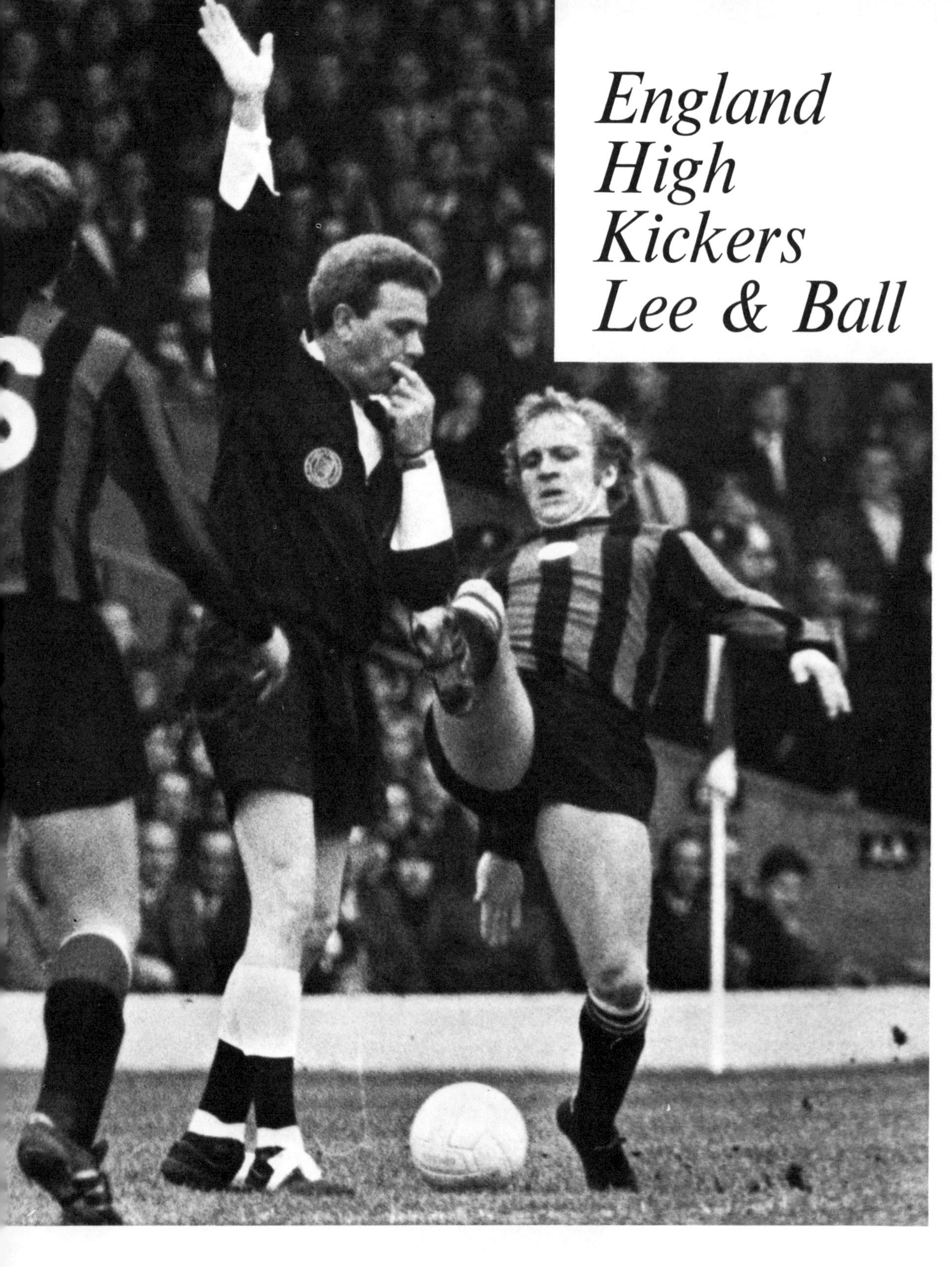

England
High
Kickers
Lee & Ball

George Best demonstrates that famous body swerve. The victim : John Hollins.

the third round. I'm prepared to put my winnings on Spurs for the championship. They are long overdue the ultimate success—but with the balance shifting towards a new soccer capital, away from the North, I am sure they will follow neighbours Arsenal to a title win.

Liverpool, who did well enough to make most managers feel a surge of pride, might need another season to get through their transitional stage completely. Bill Shankly has worked wonders—but, even if he can drum enthusiasm into his youngsters, he can't fill them with experience.

And only the knock-backs, like the Cup final, can do that.

Their neighbours, Everton, went stale both at home and in Europe. How long that feeling will last is anybody's guess—but they need the spark of pride to awaken them. Maybe Alan Ball's ineffectiveness on his return from the rigours of Mexico was the root cause. Whatever it was the tragedy is that so much skill and flair should not be dampened by the lack of success.

Everton have grown used to the good things in soccer life. Now they are going to have to start again, right from the beginning, to burst through the barriers that are stretched across the gateways to Europe.

Manchester United, under a new boss, will have to undergo a rebuilding process as vast and as far reaching as that planned and successfully executed by Bill Shankly. Will they be back on their familiar paths into Europe within the next five years? It's a fascinating question.

Will Manchester City, so often spectacular and exciting, attack and attack to storm the bastions of the league championship in their former frightening style? Or is some new planning needed at Maine Road?

I know that both Joe Mercer and coach Malcolm Allison would have liked Ralph Coates and were disappointed when he went to Spurs. I can see why. Coates, most fans' idea, of the absolute professional, dedicated, skilful, fast and brave, could probably have given City the zest they have lacked.

It goes without saying that Leeds United will be thereabouts; both in the league and the Cup. It's impossible to analyse why they have failed where other, apparently lesser sides, have broken through to score triumphs that have been denied the Yorkshire outfit.

The North versus South issue is always a hot talking point; it goes deeper than mere soccer pride and appreciation. As a northerner I've been reared on what I considered to be the best that football could offer.

Manchester United in their heydays . . . Manchester City's awesome attacking power of two seasons ago . . . Liverpool's old and new sides . . . and Everton's classy skills. They have been my scene.

I have scoffed at what London could offer. But not any more. Apart from Liverpool, as the emergent force in the North, I can't see any side halting Arsenal from hitting further highspots, or Spurs reaching high . . . to the very pinnacle of first division achievement.

After all, they now have one of the finest Northern skills in their line-up. Ralph Coates. That's some consolation for me.

The Alans—Whittle and Mullery.

A puff
from
Bobby
he takes
welcom
breather

DON REVIE

..will the greatest prizes elude him?

I WORKED as Don Revie's teammate on the BBC commentary line-up for the home internationals in May and despite our close association he never showed his disappointment, or grumbled about his side's failure to pick up a major domestic prize in the season that had just finished.

This, I suppose, is the mark of the man. His disappointments are his own worry, he refuses to share them out and bother other people with his problems. And he must have been mightily disappointed not to have picked up at least the first division title.

Good luck to Arsenal. They achieved a magnificent double in winning both the league championship and the FA Cup and beating off two fine sides, Leeds United and Liverpool, to do it.

But, for my money, Leeds finished up as moral champions. And during the coming season it will still be them as the most feared side in the land, not Arsenal. Leeds will still be the team to beat, the team everybody will want to beat.

I'm not sour because the title didn't come North—but with a bit more luck for Leeds and Don Revie it would most certainly have been in Yorkshire weeks before the Londoners even thought they had a

121

Paul Madeley.

Jack Charlton.

Allan Clarke

Terry Cooper.

Billy Bremner.

chance.

One or two results suddenly went awry, one or two daft things happened and one or two controversial points occurred which all, I think, threw Leeds out of their stride and, eventually as we saw, out of the running for the league crown.

But the worst thing that happened was when Billy Bremner was banished to the sidelines for so long with a nagging and persistent leg injury.

Billy is the hub of the side, the fire in its belly, the non-stop worker who never knows when he is beaten.

Don Revie seems to be fated to fall at the final hurdles; and it's a great pity that such a fine team as the one he has moulded should have suffered this way.

Of course Leeds won big trophies and important games but how they haven't won either the first division or the FA Cup by the end of the season is a mystery which will long puzzle me.

Many fine footballers are utter failures as soccer managers but Don is a notable exception. He is among the best ever seen in this country, or the world for that matter.

If this sounds like a glowing tribute to one of football's most glorious also-rans then that's precisely what it is.

Don is a fighter, a man born with the urge and the flair to win burning in him. He's had his ups and downs—and has struggled through them to hit peak achievements while, at the same time, not losing sight of his original plans. And that is simply: To do it his way.

Twenty years of personal soccer experience as a player, with revolutionary ideas and play in his make-up, gave Revie a background that combined orthodoxy with a hunger to do the unusual.

But when it has come to the big-time moments Don has been overshadowed with more than his share of rotten luck.

He shot Leicester City into the Cup Final with two semi-final goals against Portsmouth in 1949. Then, because of an injury which left him too weak even to attend at Wembley, he was forced to listen to his club's 3–1 defeat by Wolves on the radio.

After a brief stay with Hull City he moved on to Manchester City for £25,000—and established the

Mick Jones

Johnny Giles and the killer penalty touch to Manchester City's Joe Corrigan.

Revie-plan, a middle-link with Ken Barnes in the revolutionary, and new, 4–2–4 system.

He won the Footballer of the Year award, was capped for England—and got his side to Wembley. City were whacked 3–1 by Newcastle United. Don had lost out once more.

A year later he was back for a third try at the FA Cup. This time he broke the jinx and helped to see off Birmingham 3–1.

It was his fighting spirit that made him the star performer—he refused to let the past two upsets put him off his game.

City sold him to Sunderland—and they were relegated. Sunderland sold him to Leeds United—and they were relegated too. And in 1961 his career had flopped to its lowest level. But the fight, a different kind, was only just starting.

He was made Leeds United's manager—and the final, superb uphill fight was on. . .

Shrewd signings followed. A youth policy, with men like Norman Hunter, Gary Sprake, Peter Lorimer, Paul Reaney and Terry Cooper, was swung into action. And suddenly Leeds United were a team to be reckoned with and respected.

They were promoted in 1964 and in their next four seasons they finished 2nd, 2nd, 4th and 4th. Not bad for a starter in the boss's chair.

They lost out in the 1965 Cup Final, lost two semi-finals, were beaten in the 1966 Fairs Cup semi-final and in the final a year later. . .

They broke through by beating Arsenal in the League Cup final in 1968 and whipped Ferencvaros in the Fairs Cup final and took the 1968–69 first division title with the massive total of 67 points, a record.

But, once more, bad luck was hard on the trail of Revie and his men. They went for three trophies in 1969–70—and won nothing.

In 1971 they saw Arsenal catch them, draw level and finally pass them in a great finish for the first division crown. Colchester hammered them out of the FA Cup in a tremendous shock win.

How much has this upset gentleman Don? Not at all I bet. Watch his team this season.

A *farewell* *shot* from **Bobby**